ELIZABETH T RUSSELL
Madison, WI

℗ Ruly Press
www.rulypress.com

Art Law Conversations: A Surprisingly Readable Guide for Visual Artists.
Copyright © 2005 Elizabeth T Russell. Printed and bound in the United States of
America. All rights reserved. No part of this book may be reproduced in any
form or by any electronic or mechanical means including information storage
and retrieval systems without permission in writing from the publisher, except
by a reviewer, who may quote brief passages in a review to be printed in a magazine, newspaper or on the Web. Published by Ruly Press, an imprint of Harriet's
Guides, LLC, 402 Gammon Place, Suite 240, Madison, WI 53719. (608) 833-1555.
Requests for permission should be addressed to the publisher via US mail at the
address above or via email: tsdams@rulypress.com

First printing 2005

Visit our website at www.rulypress.com

ISBN 0-9766480-0-8

Library of Congress Control Number: 2005901787

Illustrations, cover and interior design by Kay Lum
Foreword by Carolyn Proeber, publisher of *Art Calendar* magazine
Author photo by Shannon McMahan

These and other trademarks appear throughout this book:

Allworth Press, Art Calendar, Austin Powers, Baltimore Ravens, Batman, Batman Forever, Billy-Bob, Caped Crusader, Cheers, Cleveland Browns, Coca-Cola, Director Connector, Dr. Evil, Fanzine, Harry Potter, Harvard, Hieros Gamos, Jif, Joker, KODAK, LA Magazine, LEXIS, Lipton, Masters at Augusta, McDonalds, National Public Radio, Nestea, Nickelodeon, Nolo, Novelty, NYRA, Penguin, Riddler, Samsonite, Second Bank of Gotham, Star Wars, Three Stooges, Tide, Tiger Woods, Tootsie, Volunteer Lawyers for the Arts, Viacom, Warner Brothers, Windows. All trademarks appearing in this book, whether listed on this page or not, are the exclusive property of their owners.

This book is intended to provide accurate and authoritative information regarding the subject matter. It is sold with the understanding that the publisher is not engaged in rendering legal, tax, accounting or other professional services. If legal advice or other expert assistance is required, the services of a competent professional must be obtained. Although the author and publisher have engaged in exhaustive research to ensure the accuracy and completeness of the information contained in this book, neither the author nor the publisher assumes any responsibility for errors, inaccuracies, omissions or inconsistencies contained in the book. Any slights against people or organizations are unintentional.

This book is not intended as legal advice. Because the law is not static, and every situation is different, neither the author nor the publisher assumes any responsibility for actions taken, or not taken, based on information contained in this book. Neither purchasing nor reading this book establishes an attorney-client relationship between the author and any such reader or purchaser of the book. All principles expressed in this book are subject to exceptions and qualifications, and may vary significantly from state to state. Once again: If legal advice or other expert assistance is required, the services of a competent professional must be obtained.

ATTENTION SCHOOLS, COLLEGES, UNIVERSITIES AND ARTS ORGANIZA-TIONS: Quantity discounts are available on bulk purchases of this book for educational training purposes, fund-raising or gift-giving. Special workbooks, booklets or book excerpts can also be created to accommodate your individual needs. For information contact the publisher via US mail at 402 Gammon Place, Suite 240, Madison, WI 53719 or via email: tsdams@rulypress.com

DEDICATION

To Ruth H. and Dorothy R.

Contents

PART III: YOUR BUSINESS

Acknowledgments

With infinite thanks, respect and gratitude to Julia Hughes, Vipin Gandra, Kristen Zorbini and April Faith-Slaker; to Carolyn Proeber, who started this whole thing; to Kay Lum; to Bridget and John Booske; to Stephanie Burris, Lucy Dams, Pam Metzger, Fran Nahabedian, Lois Rentmeester and Teri Stibb; to Bill Koepcke; and especially to my husband, Frebert, and my son, Raymond.

Foreword

Much legal trouble can be avoided by sticking to the basics: "ask permission," "get it in writing," "do unto others." Even so, there are specific procedures for asking, writing, and doing – and anyone can bump into a bad situation as easily as stepping on a tack. When those bad times happen, having a good attorney (or a lousy one!) on your side can literally change your life.

Knowledge can help protect you. However, learning about The Law can be difficult. The Law has a peculiar structure, and Legalese is a peculiar language. In the theater known as the courtroom, scripts are embellished with "wherefores," "therefores" and every "heretofore" and "thenceforth" one can imagine. Even in the various stages of rehearsing for a lawsuit (or just preparing a contract in hopes of avoiding one), it's easy to glaze over when your attorney starts to explain the strange and seemingly unfair twists of The Law.

Rare is the attorney who can explain things clearly, simply and humorously. Beth Russell has that gift. She has been writing our "Art Law" column for several years; I get the feeling that when she sits down to write her articles, she pours a cup of coffee, settles into her favorite chair, closes her door, and opens her heart. Copyright concern? "Let's chat about it." Trademark or patent question? "Not likely to affect this artist, but since you asked I'll be happy to address it."

Consignment laws … galleries and the Uniform Commercial Code … laws of privacy and painting celebrities … creating art under a pseudonym … reproducing national symbols in one's artwork … these are just a few of the topics Beth has covered. She brings The Law to life.

Betcha can't put the book down.

Carolyn Proeber
Publisher, *Art Calendar* Magazine

PREFACE

Shortly after establishing my law practice I received a telephone call from Carolyn Proeber, publisher of *Art Calendar* magazine. She was calling for permission to re-print an article I'd written for another publication. We chatted, and soon I was writing regularly for *Art Calendar*.

Over time, a funny thing happened. Visual artists wrote to the magazine saying they enjoyed my articles. It wasn't just that they appreciated the information, or found it useful. They said they actually enjoyed reading the articles.

I wondered, "Do they realize these articles are about law?"

They did. And they kept reading, so I kept writing.

As our relationship evolved, *Art Calendar* readers and I chose the topics for my articles together. They'd write to me describing legal issues they faced in their professional lives and I'd try to sort those issues out, in accurate yet understandable terms. Our give-and-take was such that my contributions to the magazine started to feel less like articles and more like...conversations.

Art Law Conversations is part textbook, part guide, part collection of tales. Most "conversations" appeared originally as articles in *Art Calendar*. Each is based upon facts and circumstances a real-life artist actually confronted. Each tells a true story.

Art Law Conversations is a starting point, not a treatise. For some artists this book will be enough. For others, and the attorneys representing them, it provides a base for further study. I have endeavored to present the content in a conversational tone using short sentences, plain English and "first person" narrative. Attempts at humor may or may not be successful; I hope the reader will award at least a few points for effort.

My message to visual artists is this. You must understand the fundamental legal concepts that govern your profession. You need not master these concepts – that's the lawyer's job. But you should build your own **art law knowledge base**, consisting of resources and information that will allow you to recognize legal issues, ask intelligent questions and know when to seek professional advice.

Art Law Conversations offers a solid foundation for your art law knowledge base. In fairness, so do other fine books on the subject. The difference between other books and this one: you might actually enjoy reading *Art Law Conversations*. Maybe you'll chuckle; maybe you'll breathe a little deeper; maybe you'll allow your shoulders to relax. And with that, maybe you'll absorb more information; maybe you'll gain more confidence.

Maybe you'll shout, "I get it! I get it! I finally, finally get it!"

Elizabeth T Russell
Madison, Wisconsin

Your Life

Death and Taxes: Estate Planning for Artists

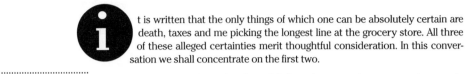

it is written that the only things of which one can be absolutely certain are death, taxes and me picking the longest line at the grocery store. All three of these alleged certainties merit thoughtful consideration. In this conversation we shall concentrate on the first two.

WILLS

FINANCIAL POWERS
OF ATTORNEY

HEALTH CARE
ADVANCE DIRECTIVES

ESTATE TAX

COPYRIGHT
(AS AN ASSET)

DISPOSITION OF
ARTISTIC WORK
AFTER DEATH

Everyone needs an estate plan. Period. It doesn't matter who you are, what you do for a living or how much money you have. Estate planning is so essential, in fact, that if you don't make a plan your state will make one for you. Let's examine some alternative scenarios.

Worst case. You have no plan whatsoever. This is like saying, "I love my government. There's no one on earth I trust more than my beloved elected officials, and whatever they decide to do with my children and everything I own is AOK with me. Plus, I'm not too fond of my family so I feel good knowing that I've made things just as difficult and expensive for them as I possibly can."

Bad case. You've given some thought to your estate plan; maybe you even discussed it with your partner or family. But life intervened, things got busy and you never got around to taking any action. Sadly, good intentions don't count. Score another for the state.

Better case. You have a **will**. There are all kinds of reasons why having a will is better than not having a will. A will disposes of your assets as you see fit, rather than as the state prescribes. With a will you designate guardians for your children; without one, a judge makes this decision. You can create a **testamentary trust** in your will to hold and administer assets for minors and disabled beneficiaries.

With a will you choose who will administer your estate (that is, who will serve as your **executor** or **personal representative**), and you can relieve that person from having to post a surety bond. In a will you can make sure your pets are cared for. You can make charitable gifts. You can clarify funeral instructions and burial preferences. You can disinherit people who otherwise would share in the distribution of your estate! If you created a trust during your life you can (and must) use a will to "pour over" the residue of your estate into that trust.

If estate tax is likely to be a concern, you can use a will to create dispositive schemes that will reduce your estate's tax liability. **Example:** Thanks to the Federal "unlimited marital deduction" you can leave your entire estate to your spouse, estate-tax free. When estate tax is an issue, however, leaving everything outright to the spouse is almost never a good idea. Why? Because even though there would be no estate tax due on the first death, the estate of the surviving spouse will contain the assets of both spouses and, at the survivor's death, the marital deduction is not available because the survivor has no spouse. So the estate of the surviving spouse, essentially, gets socked with the estate tax bill for both estates. A carefully drafted will can avoid this result. (Survivor remarried? Behold yet another reason for having a good will: to make sure subsequent spouses don't inherit your estate.)

Even better case. In addition to your will you've also executed a **financial power of attorney** and a **health care advance directive**. Different states have different names for these types of insruments but the concepts, in general, are the same. In both, you appoint someone you trust to act in your place while you are still alive but incapacitated or otherwise unable to make your own decisions. Estate planning doesn't just address what happens after your death. It's equally important (if not more so) to make sure that someone can carry on your day-to-day business matters and make health care decisions that are consistent with your wishes, if you are not able to act for yourself. (Note: in most states financial and health care powers must be granted in separate instruments.)

Best case. You're an artist. You've executed financial and health care powers of attorney and you have a will drafted especially for your unique status as an individual whose estate includes literary or artistic work of your own creation.

We've just reached the point in our conversation where you might want to open the window; enjoy a breath of fresh air. We're going to talk about estate tax.

Estate tax draws upon three easy concepts. (Estate tax also draws upon countless unfathomable concepts, so let's stick to the three easy ones.)

> **Concept #1.** When you die, the Internal Revenue Service (IRS) gleefully adds up the value of everything you own to see if your estate is large enough for them to tax.

> **Concept #2.** The IRS values the assets in your estate as of the date of your death and at their current fair market value. (This is an oversimplification, but for purposes of conversation let's just go with it.)

> **Concept #3.** "Fair market value" means the retail price at which an item would exchange hands between a willing buyer and a willing seller.

"I love my government. There's no one on earth I trust more than my beloved elected officials, and whatever they decide to do with my children and everything I own is AOK with me."

....

Think about it. If during life an artist donates his work to charity, he only gets an income tax deduction for the value of his materials.[1] When the artist dies, however, the full fair market value of work still in his possession gets included in his estate. And there's no reduction for gallery commissions or other costs of sale, so even though his estate won't receive the fair market value when it sells the work, that full value is still included "in" his estate for estate tax purposes. (Still in love with those elected officials?)

So. You might not have any money in the bank, but if at your death you own work of your own creation, the IRS is going to use the fair market value of that work in determining the overall value of your estate. In 2011 (as of this writing) $1,000,000 worth of assets will pass free of Federal estate tax. Once the value of your estate exceeds that threshold, you've got yourself a taxable estate.

Many scoff at the thought of having a million dollar estate. When you add up the fair market value of all work in your possession, though, plus work you gave away within three years of death (26 USC §2035), plus the value of things like life insurance and home equity... suddenly it's not so funny. Market value of the work alone could push you over the limit. (And remember, market value of artistic work can skyrocket after an artist's death.) Self-described "starving" clients stare in disbelief when I report they have multi-million dollar taxable estates.

One of the planning considerations unique to artists, therefore, is knowing how to value the artistic work in your estate (see Conversation #2) and to appreciate its potentially significant effect on estate tax liability. There are plenty of things you can do to reduce or eliminate estate tax – but they're not going to happen unless you take action to establish a plan before your death.

Another planning concept unique to the creative community is that the copyright to one's work is an asset separate from the work itself, often of considerable value (17 USC §201[d]; see Conversations #11 and #17). For this reason it is important to work with an attorney who understands both copyright and estate planning.

Artists should also think about where they want their work to end up, and how it will get there. Do you want it to go to a museum? A favorite nephew? Your unmarried partner? Making sure the work is properly cared for and in appreciative hands is an important concern. With that in mind, you might want to appoint a special **art executor** in your will. And when should you actually transfer the work: now, or after your death (see Conversation #3)?

Finally, it's a good idea to round up your assets so at the time of your death the assets are all physically in the same state. This includes artwork of your own creation to which you have retained legal title. If your assets are spread out in multiple US states, your executor may have to commence probate proceedings in each of those states. If you can't bring the assets physically into a single state (as, for example, if the assets include real property), one way to avoid multiple probate proceedings is to establish a **revocable living trust** and title such assets to the trust. In my view estate planning professionals seriously over-sell living trusts and, in most cases, such trusts do little more than generate unnecessary fees for the estate planning industry. However, when you have assets in more than one state a revocable living trust is an appropriate vehicle for consolidating your estate.

[1] See Conversation #3

Death and Taxes:
Estate Planning for Artists, Part 2

relentless episodes of *Star Wars* soar to the big screen, as do untold numbers of *Harry Potter* installments. The following is my contribution to sequential storytelling: *Death and Taxes, Part 2*.

....

STATE AND FEDERAL ESTATE TAX

COPYRIGHT (NAMES, SLOGANS AND CHARACTERS)

COPYRIGHT (PUBLIC DOMAIN)

In the closing scenes of *Death and Taxes 1*, our heroes were in a jam. Artists all, they'd been dealt a crippling blow: the IRS was planning to tax all art in their estates at its **fair market value**.

Fade in. The artists are enraged. They thirst for further details, knowing that accurate information and meticulous planning are paramount. Their wily minds begin to churn.

"How," they challenge, "is the IRS ever going to know about the art in our basements?"

The artists allow themselves a round of high-fives, just as the Great and Powerful Oz[2] bellows,

"The IRS is going to find out about your art when your executor files an estate tax return!"

The artists pause for reflection, then brighten with a sudden thought.

"Do all estates have to file an estate tax return?"

Oz: "No!"

The excitement builds, the music swells.

The **executor** of an estate must file a return (IRS Form 706) whether or not any estate tax will be due, if the **decedent's** gross estate exceeds the "filing requirement" for the year of the decedent's death. Often, the filing requirement is the same as the "exclusion amount," or the amount that passes free of Federal estate tax (see footnote 4). For up-to-date information regarding the filing requirement for a particular year, consult the instructions to IRS Form 706: http://www.irs.gov/pub/irs-pdf/i706.pdf. The estate tax return is due within nine months after death, unless the executor obtains an extension.

The music modulates to a minor key, as an artist with a $250,000 house, $250,000 investments and a $500,000 life insurance policy inquires, "even if my estate won't have to pay any estate tax, my executor still has to file a return?"

Oz: "That is correct. And the return must list all of your art."

*The artists with **gross estates** under $1,000,000 go out for coffee.*

"$%^&," think the others. And then, "Who decides how much my art is worth?"

An estate tax return must report articles with "artistic or intrinsic value" owned by the decedent at the time of his or her death. The **Federal regulations** relating to estate taxes provide:

[I]f there are included among the household and personal effects articles

having marked artistic or intrinsic value of a total value in excess of $3,000 ... the appraisal of an expert or experts, under oath, shall be filed with the [estate tax] return. The appraisal shall be accompanied by a written statement of the executor containing a declaration that it is made under the penalties of perjury as to the completeness of the itemized list of such property and as to the disinterested character and the qualifications of the appraiser or appraisers.

26 CFR 20.2031-6[b]

So, a qualified appraiser retained by your executor is going to get first crack at valuation.

"What do you mean by 'first crack'?"

The IRS might disagree with your executor's appraisal reports. If the total amount in dispute equals or exceeds $20,000, your case will be referred to the IRS' National Office of Art Appraisal Services (OAAS).[3] In turn, OAAS will prepare the matter for review by the IRS Commissioner's Art Advisory Panel. The Art Advisory Panel is a group of 25 renowned art dealers and museum directors who serve without compensation. The Panel meets once or twice a year, in Washington, D.C., to evaluate the appropriateness of appraisals submitted by taxpayers and executors. OAAS provides staff support for Panel meetings and organizes written background materials for the Panelists. Such written materials will include information such as the size, medium, physical condition and provenance of the work(s), as well as market research regarding relevant public and private sales. In a single day, the Panel could review between 250 and 300 appraisals.

An estate tax return must report articles with "artistic or intrinsic value" owned by the decedent at the time of his or her death.

Following a Panel meeting, OAAS will review the Panel's conclusions and forward them to the local IRS office reviewing your return. If your executor disagrees with the Panel's conclusions, the executor may request reconsideration – but only if he or she provides new or additional evidence that was not previously available to the Panel. If OAAS accepts the new evidence, the Panel will review your case again, at its next meeting.

"But that could be another whole year, and the estate tax return has to be filed within nine months!"

Very true. Your executor must be careful to apply for and obtain extensions for filing the return.

If your executor still disagrees once the IRS formally adopts the Panelists' final recommendations, IRS lawyers become involved and then it's anybody's guess about how long it will take to resolve your estate.

"How objective are the Panels?"

The IRS insists it takes steps to ensure objectivity. Panelists, who analyze appraisals for both income tax and estate tax purposes, do not know whether a particular work was gifted for an income tax charitable deduction or whether it was part of a decedent's estate. The Panel also reviews works in alphabetical order by artist, supposedly to minimize their recognition of a taxpayer's entire collection.

"But what if the work is all part of the artist's own estate? Won't it be kind of a give-away if they review everything in alphabetical order?"

Oz: "Pay no attention to that man behind the curtain!"

In 1999 the Panel accepted 38% of the appraisals it reviewed, and recommended adjustments to 54%. The remaining 8% were returned to OAAS for "additional staff development." Most all of the recommended adjustments were in favor of the IRS.

One artist (the one who finishes her Christmas shopping in July) blurts,

> "Isn't there some way to know in advance what value the IRS is likely to assign to a particular work?"

The answer, technically, is yes. The reality, however, will preclude many executors from availing themselves of the process. If an estate includes a single item of art that has been appraised at $50,000 or more, the executor may apply for a "Statement of Value" from the IRS prior to filing the estate tax return. The executor may then rely upon that Statement. The catch, of course, is that this procedure is only available for works worth $50,000 or more, plus the IRS charges $2,500 for the service, plus it can take a year or more to receive your Statement – so again, the executor must obtain extensions of time for filing the estate tax return.

> *The camera cuts to the artists who thought they didn't need to worry about estate planning and went out for coffee. We detect a growing uneasiness.*

> "We just thought of something. Don't people have to pay state estate tax as well as Federal estate tax?"

In many states (but not all), yes. And in many cases the state estate tax exclusion amount is significantly lower than the Federal. In one of the states that borders Iowa, for example, the estate tax exclusion amount is only $675,000.

> Coffee artists: "So even though we don't owe Federal estate tax, we still might have to pay estate tax to our states? Why didn't you tell us that??"

> Oz: "Yeah, um, I gotta go." *Running away,* "Hold that balloon!"

> Coffee artists: *Rejoining the conversation,* "What's the deal?"

It's kind of a shell game. In 2001 Congress passed the Economic Growth and Tax Reconciliation Act of 2001 (EGTRA), which temporarily reduces the Federal estate tax by increasing the gross estate tax exclusion amount.[4] As the exclusion amount for Federal estate tax increases, the IRS collects fewer dollars from estate taxpayers. To make up for that revenue shortfall (i.e., to "pay for" outwardly attractive tax reform), Congress added provisions to EGTRA that gradually repeal the "state death tax credit."

> "What's the state death tax credit?"

Pre-EGTRA, a decedent's Federal estate tax bill was reduced by a credit (the "state death tax credit," or SDTC) for the payment of state death taxes. There was a ceiling on this credit, so every executor would have to determine, using an IRS table, just how much Federal credit the estate could claim for the payment of state death taxes. This "ceiling" was called the "maximum allowable state death tax credit."

In general terms, an executor would write a check for $X to the state for state estate tax, and would write another check to the IRS for Federal estate tax. The amount the executor paid to the IRS, though, would reflect a subtraction (the SDTC) of either $X or something close to $X, depending on what the maximum allowable SDTC turned out to be for that particular decedent.

Here's an example. Suppose Jane's estate paid $X in state estate taxes. Her Federal estate tax liability came to $Y, and her maximum allowable state death tax credit came to [$X-$1]. Jane's estate could then subtract [$X-$1] from her

Federal estate tax bill. Stated symbolically:

$$[\text{Jane's state estate tax bill}] = [\$X]$$

$$[\text{Jane's Federal estate tax bill}] = [\$Y] - [\$X-\$1]$$

OK, hold those thoughts. There's another important piece to the SDTC story.

Many states (thirty-seven, actually) set up their estate tax schemes so that a decedent's state bill was "coupled" to (and generally would equal) the decedent's maximum allowable state death tax credit. Instead of requiring intricate calculations like the Federal scheme, those 37 states had laws that basically said, "just pay us whatever your maximum allowable state death tax credit turns out to be." This type of scheme was called a "pick-up" tax. It provided the state with a great source of estate tax revenue, without imposing any additional tax burden on individual taxpayers.

> "We get how it provided the states with revenue, but how did it
> not impose any additional burden on the taxpayers?"

Look at it this way. The SDTC provided estates with a credit to use against Federal estate tax liability. But did the amount of that credit ever go into the estate's pocket? No. The credit was for dollars the estate actually paid out, to the state.

With a "pick-up" tax, the amount of estate tax paid to the state always equaled the Federal maximum allowable state death tax credit. So the estate would subtract that amount (i.e., take the credit) from its Federal bill. Then, however, the estate turned around and paid that same amount to the state. Accordingly, from the taxpayer's perspective, it was a wash.

Can you see the problem, for "pick-up" tax states, with repealing the Federal state death tax credit?

Recall, the "pick-up" tax states had laws that specifically referenced the Federal state death tax credit. What happens to those states, when the Federal state death tax credit equals zero? That's right. They collect…zero…in state estate taxes. The IRS collects more dollars (because the credit isn't there eating away at the final tax bill) and the states collect absolutely nothing.

In response to this potentially enormous decline in estate tax revenue, pick-up tax states are passing "decoupling" laws imposing their own separate estate tax structures. As a result, estates subject to estate tax liability will have to pay more dollars to the IRS (due to elimination of the SDTC) plus brand new estate tax dollars to the states, for which there will be no corresponding Federal credit.

In 2011, when the Federal exclusion amount falls back down to $1,000,000, taxpayers will be in the same boat as they were in 2002. Without the state death tax credit, however, and with new state tax liabilities, that boat will have sprung a serious leak.

----

[2] The books and stories L. Frank Baum have passed into the public domain (http://www.io.space ports.com/~wysardry/tales/b/baum/wizardoz/intro.htm; see Conversation #21 regarding copyright duration). Copyright, moreover, does not protect names, titles or short phrases (http://www.copyright.gov/circs/circ34.pdf) nor does it protect the names, concepts or intangible attributes of characters (http://www.copyright.gov/circs/circ44.pdf). Characters may be protected under state, common or trademark laws – but not under United States copyright law.

[3] Information about OAAS and the Art Advisory Panel was obtained for this conversation from the *Annual Summary Report for 1999* of the Art Advisory Panel of the Commissioner of Internal Revenue.

[4] EGTRA causes the Federal exclusion amount to increase from $1,000,000 in 2002 to $1,500,000 in 2004, to $2,000,000 in 2006, to $3,500,000 in 2009. In 2010 (barring intervening legislative change) there will be no Federal estate tax at all, but in 2011 the estate tax returns, with an exclusion amount of $1,000,000.

Income Tax Deductions for Donating One's Work to Charity

for years Congress has considered bills proposing a "fair market value" amendment to the Internal Revenue Code. The bills have gone nowhere.

H.R. 3249 (for example) was introduced in the United States House of Representatives during the first session of the 106th Congress, on November 8, 1999. Titled the "Artists' Contributions to American Heritage Act of 1999," the bill would have amended section 170(e) of the Internal Revenue Code to permit an income tax deduction equal to fair market value for charitable contributions of literary, musical, artistic or scholarly compositions created by the donor. Representative Amo Houghton of New York stated in introductory remarks that the bill would "significantly enhance the ability of museums and public libraries to acquire important original works by artists, writers and composers, and ensure the preservation of these works for future generations."

....

INCOME TAX
CHARITABLE
DEDUCTION

COST BASIS

ORDINARY INCOME

FAIR MARKET VALUE

GAIN

Although the bill had 59 co-sponsors, it died, as have subsequent, similar bills. Apparently a majority of our elected representatives aren't so very concerned after all, with American Heritage.

Once upon a time, artists could deduct the **fair market value** of works they donated to charity. Tax reform in 1969 put an end to that, ostensibly in order to prevent artist-donors from racking up charitable deductions by overestimating the value of their work. Current law doesn't come right out and say, "you can only deduct the cost of materials for work you donate to charity," so if you go looking for those words you're not going to find them. (And indeed, I hope you have better things to do than curl up with the Internal Revenue Code on a chilly winter's eve). But that's the reality. You can only deduct your **cost basis**, which in most cases means the cost of materials you used to create the work.

If you're satisfied with that explanation, turn the page and go on with your life. If you want proof, read on. But remember…you asked for it.

A Reader points to IRS Publication 561, which sets forth procedure for determining the value of donated property. Reader notes:

> *There's no clarification here about artists donating work, but it clearly says that work valued at less than $5000 can be deducted at the Fair Market Value without a supporting appraisal. Perhaps there's some other place in the publications that states that artists can only deduct the cost of materials for work they donate, but I can't find it, even though I know that has been the rule for decades.*

Although Reader is correct in several respects, the controlling phrase in her comment is "without a supporting appraisal." Publication 561 advises when an appraisal is or is not required, for the donation of material that otherwise qualifies for a fair market value deduction. If we donate something for which we are, in the first place, entitled to take a fair market value deduction, we need an appraisal only if the value of the item equals or exceeds $5000. If we aren't entitled to take a fair market value deduction at all, though, Publication 561 is not relevant.

And that, of course, is the case for artists. Individuals who "trade" in creativity may not deduct the value of their own labor, thus they are not entitled to take a fair market value (FMV) deduction when they donate their work to charity. Does it say that specifically in a provision I can cite? No. But a combination of Internal Revenue Code provisions, Internal Revenue Regulations and case law supports this irrefutable conclusion.

Creative property is **ordinary income** property in the hands of the creator. That means, the creative property does not qualify as a **capital asset**, so when such property is sold it will generate "ordinary income" as opposed to long-term capital gain (26 USC §§170; 1221).

Internal Revenue regulations define "ordinary income property" to include:

> ...*property held by the donor primarily for sale to customers in the ordinary course of his trade or business; a work of art created by the donor; a manuscript prepared by the donor; letters and memoranda prepared by or for the donor....*

26 CFR §1.170A-4(b)(1)

Because creative property is ordinary income in the hands of the creator, the income tax charitable deduction attributable to such property is limited to the creator's basis in the property. See 26 USC §170(a). In simplified terms, one's "basis" equals the number of dollars one actually spent to create or acquire the property.

When ordinary income property is sold, income tax is due on the transaction's "gain."

Gain is calculated by reducing the ordinary income property's fair market value by the taxpayer's basis in the property. (FMV-Basis=Gain)

The income tax charitable deduction under IRC §170(a) is reduced by the "gain" that would have occurred in a sale; thus only the donor's basis is deductible (FMV-Gain=Basis)

Individuals who "trade" in creativity may not deduct the value of their own labor, thus they are not entitled to take a fair market value (FMV) deduction when they donate their work to charity.

And *voila*: no FMV deduction when you donate art of your own creation to charity.

The constitutionality of this scheme as applied to artists has been upheld (*Maniscalco* v. *Commissioner of Internal Revenue*, 632 F 2d 6 [6th Cir. 1980]), so a legislative amendment will be necessary to correct the inequity.

So far in this conversation we've been talking about charitable gifts you make during your lifetime. The rules are totally different if you donate your work in your will, and the transfer takes place after your death.

Let's say you wish to donate a work of art that you created. If you donate that work to charity, as we just established, your charitable deduction is limited to your basis. If you donate the work in your will, however, your gross estate gets reduced by the full amount of the gift (26 USC §2055). Stated otherwise: if you wait and donate the work when you die, your estate gets an estate tax deduction for the full fair market value whereas if you make the donation during life you get an income tax deduction equal only to your basis in the work.

Let's take this one step further. (And again, please understand that this entire conversation has been extremely simplified. For advice specific to your situation you must consult a tax specialist.) Suppose you want to give away a piece of your art to a person or organization (e.g., a friend or a local business) that does not qualify as a charity. In such case, of course, charitable deductions are not available, but there are other tax concerns. When you gift a work to a non-charitable donee, during your life, the donee acquires your basis in the work (26 USC §1015). If the work is currently valued at $50,000 and your basis is $200, the donee assumes your $200 basis. When the donee ultimately sells that work, therefore, the donee is going to have a significant taxable gain for purposes of income tax. (Remember: FMV – Basis = Gain.)

If, however, you gift the work to that same donee through your will, the donee gets a "step-up in basis" to the work's fair market value (26 USC §1014). That saves the donee a whole lot of income tax when the donee sells the work, because the donee's taxable gain is only the difference between the sale price and $50,000, rather than the difference between the sale price and (had the donee acquired your basis) $200.

Prior to EGTRA (see Conversation #2) the step-up in basis rules provided artists planning their estates with meaningful and significant tax-saving alternatives. But there's bad news. Pursuant to EGTRA, the step-up in basis rules are going away. For decedents dying after December 31, 2009, property acquired from a decedent will be treated in the same manner as though it had been transferred during the decedent's life (26 USC §1022). In other words, after December 31, 2009, you can gift the work during life or you can gift it under your will and the non-charitable donee will acquire your basis, either way.

But enough of this shell game. Let's move on to the legal issues affecting your work.

Your Work

Photographing Your Work: Who Owns the Rights?

 photographer recently claimed he owned rights to my artwork because he photographed it. He believes his skill in photography gives him some rights of entitlement. I see it differently. I always maintained that I hold all copyrights to my work, even if it is photographed. Please tell me where the law stands. Is this a gray area?

COPYRIGHT BASICS

WORK OF AUTHORSHIP

BUNDLE OF RIGHTS

DERIVATIVE WORK

LICENSING

The odds of any legal issue being "gray" are usually pretty good. Reader's question, though, provides a most unusual opportunity. I can say, "This isn't a gray area at all!" The issue is complicated, yes. But once sorted out it's pretty clear.

Let us begin with some copyright basics.

Material subject to copyright protection is generally referred to as "work of authorship." If you create copyrightable material, you are its "author" even if the rest of the world considers you a painter, sculptor, architect, composer, playwright, etc.

Copyright law tells us what types of work qualify as "works of authorship" (17 USC §102[a]; see Figure 1.). Among other categories of creative expression, "pictorial, graphic and sculptural works" are protected as works of authorship (17 USC §102[a][5]). Paintings, drawings, photographs and other visual art fall into this category (see Copyright Office instructions for registering visual art, at http://www.copyright .gov/register/visual.html).

When one acquires a copyright, one really acquires a "bundle" of six independent rights (17 USC §106; see Figure 1. The Copyright Act is available at the Copyright Office website: http://www.copyright.gov/title17/ and the entire United States Code is searchable online at: http://uscode .house.gov/ search/criteria.php).

> **Material subject to copyright protection is generally referred to as "work of authorship." If you create copyrightable material, you are its "author" even if the rest of the world considers you a painter, sculptor, architect, composer, playwright, etc.**

TITLE 17 OF THE *UNITED STATES CODE*
WORKS OF AUTHORSHIP AND THE BUNDLE OF RIGHTS

§ 102. Subject matter of copyright: In general

(a) Copyright protection subsists, in accordance with this title, in original works of authorship fixed in any tangible medium of expression, now known or later developed, from which they can be perceived, reproduced, or otherwise communicated, either directly or with the aid of a machine or device. Works of authorship include the following categories:

    (1) literary works;

    (2) musical works, including any accompanying words;

    (3) dramatic works, including any accompanying music;

    (4) pantomimes and choreographic works;

    (5) pictorial, graphic, and sculptural works;

    (6) motion pictures and other audiovisual works;

    (7) sound recordings; and

    (8) architectural works.

(b) In no case does copyright protection for an original work of authorship extend to any idea, procedure, process, system, method of operation, concept, principle, or discovery, regardless of the form in which it is described, explained, illustrated, or embodied in such work.

§ 106. Exclusive rights in copyrighted works

Subject to sections 107 through 122, the owner of copyright under this title has the exclusive rights to do and to authorize any of the following:

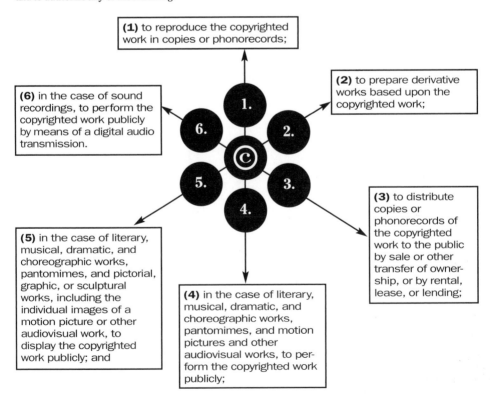

(1) to reproduce the copyrighted work in copies or phonorecords;

(2) to prepare derivative works based upon the copyrighted work;

(3) to distribute copies or phonorecords of the copyrighted work to the public by sale or other transfer of owner-ship, or by rental, lease, or lending;

(4) in the case of literary, musical, dramatic, and choreographic works, pantomimes, and motion pictures and other audiovisual works, to per-form the copyrighted work publicly;

(5) in the case of literary, musical, dramatic, and choreographic works, pantomimes, and pictorial, graphic, or sculptural works, including the individual images of a motion picture or other audiovisual work, to display the copyrighted work publicly; and

(6) in the case of sound recordings, to perform the copyrighted work publicly by means of a digital audio transmission.

I like to think of a copyright as a pile of firewood, and each of the six "§106" rights as separate logs on the pile. The copyright owner can license away one or more of the "logs," and still retain the rest of the pile. That is, you do not "lose" your copyright just because you permit another party to exercise one or more of your rights under §106.

One of the six rights is the right "to reproduce the copyrighted work in copies or phonorecords" (17 USC §106[1]); another is the right "to prepare derivative works based upon the copyrighted work" (17 USC § 106[2]).

> Note: there has been much debate whether, when one photographs a copyrighted work, one is creating a "copy" (§106[1]) or a "derivative work" (§106[2]). If the photograph contains a sufficient amount of creativity (see Conversation #18), it's a derivative work (see Copyright Office Circular 14 at http://www.copyright.gov/circs/circ14.pdf). If not, it's just a copy. Either way, the photographer needs a license from the owner of the underlying, copyrighted work. For purposes of this conversation we will assume that the photograph is a "derivative" of the copyrighted work.

With these thoughts in mind, let's return to Reader's question.

Reader did not specify his artistic medium. Let's assume it's paint on canvas, and call him "Painter."

OK. Painter creates his painting. As its author, Painter owns the copyright to the painting. Painter's copyright includes all six of the §106 rights, including the right to prepare derivative works based upon the painting.

Painter needs photos of the painting for his portfolio, so Painter hires Photographer. Recall the six rights. Without a **license** (i.e., permission) from Painter, Photographer cannot shoot the painting. Why? Because the resulting photos would be derivative works based upon the painting. Taking the photos without a license would violate Painter's exclusive right under §106(2) and, thus, would constitute copyright infringement.

So first, Photographer needs a license from Painter to photograph the painting. Painter and Photographer should have a written agreement, setting forth the terms and the scope of Photographer's license to shoot the painting. If they do not, i.e., if they have only a verbal agreement that Photographer will do the shoot, it can be inferred that Painter has granted Photographer a limited, **nonexclusive license** to take the photos.

Derivative works are separately copyrightable and, to the extent of the author's creative contributions, afford the author the full range of §106 rights.

Query #1. At this point, who holds what rights with respect to the painting?

Well, Photographer has a license to take photos of, and thus to prepare derivative works of, the painting. If Painter granted Photographer an **exclusive license** to do this, no one other than Photographer could photograph the painting, for the purposes specified, during the term of the license. If Photographer's license is "nonexclusive," Painter is free to license this right to others beside Photographer, at any time. (Note: exclusive licenses must be in writing.)

Painter still owns and controls all the other §106 "logs" of his copyright, subject only to the license he granted to Photographer. For example, Painter still retains the right to license copies of the painting for various purposes, to display the painting publicly, to reproduce it in other media, etc. The only thing Painter can't do is violate the specific terms of Photographer's license.

Query #2. Who owns what rights with respect to the photographs?

Recall, we are assuming that the photographs contain sufficient originality (in their composition, lighting, etc.) to be derivative works based upon the painting. As such, Photographer owns a copyright interest in the photographs. That interest is limited, however, to the creative elements that Photographer herself contributed to the photographs. Photographer does not own and has not acquired any copyright interest in the underlying work (the painting). Consequently, if Photographer wishes to use the photos for any purpose in the future, Photographer will still need a license from Painter.[5]

Query #3. Does Painter have any copyright interest in the photographs?

It depends, but probably not. Unless Photographer specifically (and in writing) "assigned" copyright in the photographs to Painter, Painter cannot exercise any of the §106 rights, with respect to the photos, without Photographer's permission. Why? Because Photographer holds a copyright interest in the photos. Yes, it's limited in scope to composition and lighting, but that counts. Derivative works are separately copyrightable and, to the extent of the author's creative contributions, afford the author (here, Photographer) the full range of §106 rights. If Painter wished to reproduce or display the photos, therefore, he would need Photographer's permission to do so even though his own work constituted the subject of the photographs.

> **Anyone who seeks to use a derivative work must obtain an appropriate license from whoever holds a copyright interest in the derivative AND from the copyright holder(s) of any work upon which the derivative was based.**

Query #4. (This is my favorite query.) What happens if a third party comes to Photographer and asks for permission to display or otherwise exercise one or more of the §106 rights with respect to the photos?

In this case, the third party would need a license from Photographer (because Photographer has a copyright interest in the photos) and from Painter, because Painter's copyrighted material appears in the photos. **Write this down:** Anyone who seeks to use a derivative work must obtain an appropriate license from whoever holds a copyright interest in the derivative AND from the copyright holder(s) of any work upon which the derivative was based.

So, Reader, you have not "lost" your copyright. Photographer has no rights at all in or to your artwork. But Photographer does hold a limited copyrightable interest in the derivative works (i.e., the photographs) she created. Perhaps this will clear things up:

If you are	**Painter**	**Photographer**	**A Third Party**
…and you want to use the painting… you need permission from:	Nobody	Painter	Painter
…and you want to use the photographs… you need permission from:	Photographer	Painter	Photographer AND Painter

Copyright is a twisted trail. With respect to any particular work, we must often pursue multiple paths to sort out who controls what, and then to obtain appropriate licenses from everyone with a copyrightable interest in the work. It's complicated. But not gray.

---

[5] Would Photographer need a license to use her own photos if the subject of her photos was something uncopyrightable like, for example, a river? No. The only reason Photographer needs a license, in this case, is because her photos are derivative works of copyrightable material: the painting.

Giving Teeth to Copyright Law: The *Billy-Bob* Story

s savvy Readers you undoubtedly know there's been breaking news in the industry. I refer, of course, to the industry that designs and manufactures novelty teeth.

The United States Court of Appeals for the Seventh Circuit issued a fascinating copyright decision in the matter of *Billy-Bob Teeth, Inc.* v. *Novelty, Inc.* (329 F3d 586, 7th Cir. 2003), prefacing its opinion with the following:

> When "International Man of Mystery" Austin Powers gazes at the comely British agent Kensington and purrs "groovy Baby" or "oh behave!" he always smiles, exposing a set of teeth that the best orthodontist in the world could not improve. They are ugly, and therein lies their beauty, at least from a financial point of view. This…case involves "novelty" teeth – oversized, crooked, and chipped teeth that fit over a person's real teeth. People wear them to get a laugh. Actor Mike Myers wore them when, as Austin Powers, he foiled the dia-bolical plans of Dr. Evil to achieve world domination.

The **plaintiffs** in *Billy-Bob* were two friends. One of them (a dental student) designed a set of novelty teeth as a joke. The other friend saw the teeth, laughed like crazy and realized immediately that the teeth could generate serious cash. The two friends went into business, marketed the teeth and soon cleared $5 million per year in sales.

At one point the **defendant**, Novelty, Inc., contacted Billy-Bob, Inc. to obtain samples of the teeth, purportedly because Novelty wished to sell and distribute the Billy-Bob product. Billy-Bob sent the samples. Soon thereafter, Novelty told Billy-Bob they weren't interested after all. As savvy Readers you can guess what happened next: Novelty started marketing its own teeth.

The Novelty teeth were remarkably similar to Billy-Bob's, though allegedly of inferior quality. Billy-Bob sued for copyright infringement, and ultimately prevailed.

So what does *Billy-Bob* mean for the savvy Reader?

Copyright Protection for Three-Dimensional Art

This case answers a question I frequently hear from jewelry artists, sculptors and others who create three dimensional art: is such work copyrightable? Yes. If sufficiently original (see Conversation #18) it's copyrightable under section 102 of the United States Copyright Law as "pictorial, graphic, and sculptural work" (17 USC §102[5]; see Figure 1). However, copyright protection for such work only extends to aspects of the work that are non-utilitarian:

> Copyright does not protect the mechanical or utilitarian aspects of … works of craftsmanship. It may, however, protect any pictorial, graphic, or sculptural authorship that can be identified separately from the utilitarian aspects of an object. Thus, a useful article may have both copyrightable and uncopy-rightable features. For example, a carving on the back of a chair or a floral relief design on silver flatware could be protected by copyright, but the design of the chair or flatware itself could not.

Copyright Office Circular 40, "Copyright Registration for Works of the Visual Arts" at http://www.copyright.gov/circs/circ 40.pdf

Registration Basics. Looking at Billy-Bob's actual copyright registrations, online, is a good exercise. Go to the Copyright Office website (http://www.copyright.gov) and click on "Search Records." Then click on "Books, Music, etc.," select the "Author" radio button and enter "Billy Bob Teeth" (without the quotation marks). You'll see there are three items listed for "Billy Bob Teeth, Inc." Select that box, select the "Full-Record Display" radio button, and click "Submit."

Note the first registration, number VA-771-490. Here are two good practices if you're submitting an application to protect art that's affixed to a useful article. Look at the "Title" and "Description" fields. Billy-Bob was careful to claim copyright protection only for elements of the teeth that are, in fact, eligible for copyright protection. As the "Note" section observes, "applicant states no claim is made on functional design of teeth." Make such a statement on your application.

Now look at the second registration, number VA-771-491. This is actually a "derivative work" based on the original design (VA-771-490). VA-771-491 takes the original design and adds a chip in the second tooth from the right. The registration identifies the original design (VA-771-490) as "pre-existing material" and limits its claim on the derivative to the "new matter," i.e., the chip. This is proper practice when applying to register a derivative work.

It's important to obtain separate copyright registrations for individual pieces, both derivatives and completely original works (see Conversation #17). Again, Billy-Bob, Inc. acted properly, filing separate applications for "Sculpture and Artwork in Novelty Teeth," "Sculpture and Artwork in Novelty Teeth with Chip," and "Sculpture and Artwork in Novelty Teeth with Cavity."

Copyright protects original works of authorship that are fixed in any tangible medium of expression

Must you register your work in order to "get" a copyright? No. Copyright attaches as soon as copyrightable material is put into a "fixed form." Registration has many benefits, however, such as making you eligible for **statutory damages** in the event of infringement (see Conversations #15 and #17).

Intellectual Property Basics. *Billy-Bob* also prompts discussion about differentiating among the three primary types of intellectual property: copyright, trademark and patent. Every artist should know how to tell one from the other.

Copyright protects original works of authorship that are fixed in any tangible medium of expression (17 USC §102; see Figure 1). Copyright protects expression. It does not protect ideas, methods or systems. It protects one's expression of an idea, but not the idea itself (see Conversation #6). It protects the expression of art affixed to an otherwise useful article, but it does not protect the article. Copyright does not protect names, titles, slogans or formulas (see footnote, Conversation #2).

In *Billy-Bob,* certain artistic aspects of the teeth were protected by copyright, as sculptural expression. As a mechanical means for covering one's natural teeth, however, the teeth themselves were not copyrightable. Novelty, Inc. ran afoul of the Copyright Act not because it produced teeth, but because the teeth it produced infringed upon the artistic expression that was fixed in Billy-Bob's products.

Trademark identifies the source of goods and services (see Conversation #23). Trademark law exists to protect consumers by preventing deceptive and misleading uses of marks in the marketplace. Trademark law protects single words, slogans, names, drawings, logos, packaging, etc., as long as the mark in question serves as an indicator of source.

A secondary issue in *Billy-Bob* was **trade dress** (see Conversation #24), i.e., the extent to which the packaging of Novelty, Inc. teeth so closely resembled the packaging of Billy-Bob teeth that a consumer would likely confuse the Novelty, Inc. product for a Billy-Bob product. (Billy-Bob was also successful on this point, for legal reasons unrelated to this conversation.)

Patent grants an inventor the right to exclude others from making, using, selling or importing her invention (see Conversation #6). Unlike copyright, patent's express purpose is to protect useful things like machines and processes. (And in the interest of completeness I shall report without further elaboration that patent also protects asexually reproduced plants.)

Although patent wasn't at issue in *Billy-Bob*, let's pretend it was. I mentioned earlier that Novelty, Inc.'s trouble had nothing to do with the fact it produced teeth, because copyright doesn't protect the "thing" itself, if it happens to be a useful article.

(Notwithstanding one's personal views on the usefulness of novelty teeth, they are for purposes of legal analysis, "useful.")

Novelty was free to make ugly teeth as long as the appearance of its teeth didn't infringe upon the copyrightable artistic expression fixed in Billy-Bob teeth. Had Billy-Bob obtained a patent, however, Novelty would have been precluded from manufacturing any teeth, regardless of their appearance, to the extent Novelty's teeth infringed upon the numbered "claims" set forth in Billy-Bob's patent.

Patent law is extremely complicated. So much so, in fact, that patent lawyers have to be admitted to a special bar and most hold advanced degrees in scientific disciplines. For a general overview (which is likely to be more than you'll ever want) consult the United States Patent and Trademark Office website (http://www.uspto.gov/).

To sum up:

• Copyright protects expression

• Trademark identifies the source of goods and services

• Patent protects useful machines, processes and asexually reproduced plants

• Novelty items can make you rich

> **Novelty was free to make ugly teeth as long as the appearance of its teeth didn't infringe upon the copyrightable artistic expression fixed in Billy-Bob teeth.**

Protecting Ideas

 created an art using mixed media. I will admit that it is rather easy to create but the outcome is beautiful. My fear is, I sell one and someone recreates it, makes others and makes money from them. How can I protect my idea?

I am a furniture maker and am completing a new chair design. How can I protect my ideas from being used by other furniture makers?

How does one protect an idea?

At least initially, keep it to yourself. If you share an artistic idea with a friend, and you have not yet reduced that idea to a tangible medium of expression, your friend can run out and use the idea and there's not a thing in the world you can do about it.

Let's apply this to our Reader who invented the mixed media technique. For simplicity's sake, and with deep apologies to Reader, let's say the technique consists of gluing macaroni to cardboard. The technique starts out as an idea in Reader's brain. As long as it remains in Reader's brain, it is safe and protected. Not so, once she shares with others. Consider the following scenarios.

Scenario #1. Reader has not yet created any actual work; she has glued nary a noodle to cardboard. When Max comes over for tea, Reader tells Max about her idea. Max excuses himself, goes home and empties his pasta pantry, creates a glorious work of art and sells it for a million dollars. Too bad for Reader; ideas are not copyrightable.

Scenario #2. Reader made a prototype and showed it to Max. Once again, Max went home, made his own piece of macaroni art and earned millions. Here's where things get sticky.

Reader's work, itself, acquired copyright protection the minute she fixed her expression in a tangible medium. In other words, when she glued the first piece of macaroni to cardboard, the resulting expression was protected by copyright. Reader's work reflected her own original expression. Such expression included, for example, how she positioned individual pieces of pasta on the cardboard base; how she used color, texture, etc. Copyright protected her expression. Copyright did not protect the idea of making art by gluing macaroni to cardboard. Whether Max's work infringed upon Reader's, therefore, depends on whether Max's work copied protectible elements of Reader's expression. If Max's expression (positioning, color, texture, etc.) was original and did not infringe on Reader's expression, he did nothing wrong.

 So copyright does not protect ideas. (Nor does it protect procedures, processes, useful articles, systems, concepts, methods of operation, principles or discoveries.) Copyright only protects original expression in a fixed form, and its protection extends only to statutorily-defined "works of authorship" (see Figure 1). The following Copyright Office publications are instructive on these points:

Circular 31: Ideas, Methods or Systems
http://www.copyright.gov/circs/circ31.pdf

COPYRIGHT
(ORIGINAL
EXPRESSION)

COPYRIGHT (IDEAS,
METHODS, SYSTEMS,
USEFUL ARTICLES)

PATENT

Factsheet FL-103: Useful Articles
http://www.copyright.gov/fls/fl103.pdf

But copyright is not the only game in town.

Copyright is only one branch of intellectual property. Other branches, each of which protects a different type of intellectual property, include patent, trademark and trade secrets (see Conversation #5). Under certain circumstances artists can use patent law to protect their work when copyright is not available or would not provide adequate protection.[6]

There are three types of patents. A **utility patent** may be granted to anyone "who invents or discovers any new and useful process, machine, article of manufacture, or composition of matter, or any new and useful improvement thereof." A **design patent** may be granted to anyone "who invents a new, original, and ornamental design for an **article of manufacture;**" and a **plant patent** may be granted to anyone "who invents or discovers and asexually reproduces any distinct and new variety of plant." (Basic Facts About Patents: http://www.uspto.gov/main/patents.htm).

Regarding design patents, the United States Patent and Trademark Office explains:

> A design consists of the visual ornamental characteristics embodied in, or applied to, an article of manufacture. Since a design is manifested in appearance, the subject matter of a design patent application may relate to the configuration or shape of an article, to the surface ornamentation applied to an article, or to the combination of configuration and surface ornamentation. A design for surface ornamentation is inseparable from the article to which it is applied and cannot exist alone. It must be a definite pattern of surface ornamentation, applied to an article of manufacture.
>
> In discharging its patent-related duties, the United States Patent and Trademark Office (USPTO or Office) examines applications and grants patents on inventions when applicants are entitled to them. The patent law provides for the granting of design patents to any person who has invented any new, original and ornamental design for an article of manufacture. A design patent protects only the appearance of the article and not structural or utilitarian features.
>
> Guide to Filing a Design Patent Application:
> http://www.uspto.gov/web/ offices /pac/design/

Pursuing a design or utility patent might be an alternative for our furniture-making Reader to consider.

Patent law is extraordinarily complex, so if you are considering patent law as a means for protecting your work, consult with an attorney admitted to practice before the United States Patent and Trademark Office (see Conversation #5).

As artists our natural inclination is to think in terms of copyright as the exclusive means for protecting our work.

------

[6] An interesting website regarding patent law and its application to art is: Patenting Art and Entertainment http://www.patenting-art.com/

Using Copyrighted Material in Your Work

Outstanding artists continue to labor under copyright myths, legends and downright falsehoods. Artists must erase these myths from their minds, else place their work and their very livelihoods in peril.

The greatest myth of all is that an artist may use another's copyrighted image as long as she changes the image by some magical degree or percentage. Not true!

There is no bright line, across-the-board rule that permits you to use a copyrighted image as long as you change it "enough." Rather (in the time-honored tradition of legal convolution), the only way to know whether you may use a copyrighted image is to apply a complete legal analysis to every image you use. It's tedious; it's a pain; and if you work with an attorney (which I strongly recommend) it costs money. On the other hand, this is your business and clearing the rights to your work should be worth the investment.

Wait. A complete legal analysis for every single image?

"What the $%^& does that mean?"

"How am I supposed to do that?"

"Are you $%^& crazy? I'm a collage artist!"

It is daunting, so go ahead and vent. Do what you must to overcome hating the fact that you have to deal with this. Then take a deep breath, remember all the warm and fuzzy things you love about the United States Constitution, and read on.

There are six fundamental questions you need to ask (and answer) when you want to use someone else's image in your work. There are countless sub-issues related to each of the six questions, and that's why you should work with a lawyer. Still, there is good reason to study the six questions and their underlying concepts. With an informed appreciation for the issues, you'll be in good shape either to clear the rights on your own or to streamline your work with an attorney.

Question number one: **Is the image you want to use copyrightable material?** Not everything is subject to copyright protection. If the image isn't copyrightable at all, your analysis ends and at least from a copyright perspective, you can use the image. Simple! What's not so simple is the fact that there are volumes of caselaw discussing what is and what is not copyrightable. (Remember those countless sub-issues…?) To be copyrightable the image must qualify as a "work of authorship" under the Copyright Act (17 USC §102; see Figure 1). The image must also be "original" and "fixed in a tangible medium of expression."

Second question: Assuming the image is copyrightable **is it in the public domain?** If the image is in the public domain, you can use it. Simple! What's not so simple is calculating when specific images fall into the public domain (see Conversation #21). At the Copyright Office website, Circular 15a addresses the issue of copyright duration (http://www.copyright.gov/circs/circ15a.pdf). Public domain calculations can be extremely tricky, so if more is at stake than you can afford to lose, be sure to consult with a copyright attorney.

OK. The image is copyrightable and not in the public domain. Question number three is painfully obvious, yet frequently overlooked: **do you have permission to**

use the image? If you have permission, you can use the image as long as your use complies with the terms of the agreement. Always get permissions and licenses in writing. Simple!

No permission? Then move on to question number four: **would your use of the image be an infringement of the owner's copyright?** We mentioned above that not all material is copyrightable. In the same vein, not all uses of copyrighted material are infringements. Unfortunately this is where myth has muddied the waters. Many artists believe that a minimal amount of copying is OK, and that if one changes an image in "X" manner or to "Y" degree, then using the image is not a legal infringement. This is not true. Determining whether your use is or is not an infringement requires the meticulous application of "tests" that have been formulated over the years by various Federal courts (see Conversation #19). You must apply these tests to every proposed use of every image you want to use. And that's the good news! Federal courts sitting in different parts of the country devise their own tests – so before you can sit down and apply the tests to your images, you first need to figure out which tests to use!

Artists can (and should) learn to answer many of their own legal questions. In my view, however, analyzing an image for copyright infringement falls into the category of "don't try this at home." A better use of the artist's time is to create and maintain an "image log." Dedicate a page in your log for each image you want to use. Include a copy or an accurate description of the image; note where you found the image (the "source"); note who owns the copyright on the image and who owns the copyright on the source; and collect any other copyright-related information you can gather. Describe your proposed use of the image. Then hire a copyright lawyer to do the infringement analysis. If you come prepared with an accurate, well-organized log, you'll cut down on time the lawyer will need to spend researching your case, and that will help keep your costs in check.

(Note: the downside to keeping a log is that it's a tangible record of your diligence [or lack thereof] that could potentially be used against you in litigation. As always, consult with your own attorney for advice specific to your situation.)

Back to the six questions. Assuming infringement, question number five asks, **can you assert "fair use?"** Legal scholars debate whether fair use is a defense to infringement or whether, if fair use exists, by definition there cannot have been infringement in the first place. Like you, I have little tolerance for legal scholars, so consider this reality: if we're talking fair use, you've already been sued – and that's not good. Whether you're legally right or wrong, you do not want to be sued. Ever. Defending a Federal lawsuit is so expensive that once you've been sued: you lose. If you're going to rely on fair use, therefore, you need to be thinking ahead about the context in which it is likely to arise. Who has the stronger case: You, for fair use? Or the copyright owner, for infringement? You'll never know for sure, but in deciding initially whether to use an image, you should factor in the likelihood of eventual litigation.

Fair use is a multi-step balancing test in which no single factor is determinative. (See Copyright Office Factsheet FL-102 at http://www.copyright.gov/fls/fl102.html) The first factor to consider is the "purpose and character" of your use. Are you using the image for a commercial purpose, or for an educational or expressive purpose? In general, educational/expressive purposes cut in favor of fair use while commercial purposes cut against. Is your use of the image "transformative" (do you add your own creative elements), or do you simply re-create the original image? In general, transformative uses cut in favor of fair use; re-creation cuts against.

Next, you need to examine the nature of the image itself. Was it the product of someone's creative energies? Or was it more a work of diligence? In general, the more creative the image, the more protection it will receive and the less likely you are to make a case for fair use. Was the image published (less protection) or not published (more protection); is it by nature entertaining (more protection) or educational (less protection)? A court will also weigh how much of the image you use (varying amounts might be permissible, depending on the nature of the image itself) and the effect of your use on the market for the original image. At the risk of sounding like a defective sound recording, you're much better off working with an attorney than trying to master fair use on your own.

Question number six: **do you have any other defenses to infringement?** Fair use is not the only defense to infringement. Assuming you've struck out on questions one through five, your last hope for using a copyrighted image (and staying out of trouble) is to establish an alternative defense to infringement. The defense of "independent creation," for example, is available if you can establish that you did not copy the copyrighted work and that, in fact, any similarity between your work and the protected work is purely coincidental. Another possible defense: you copied, but you did not copy any protected elements of the copyrighted work.

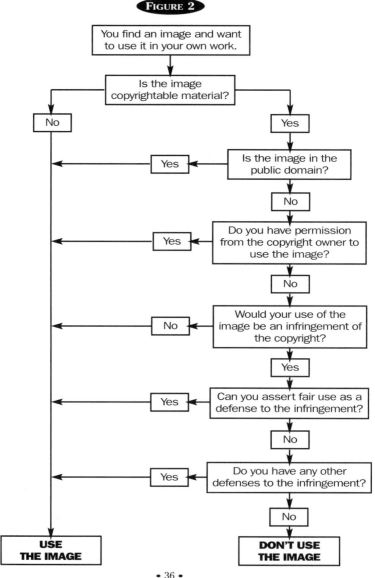

FIGURE 2

You find an image and want to use it in your own work.

Is the image copyrightable material?

No

Yes

Is the image in the public domain?

Yes

No

Do you have permission from the copyright owner to use the image?

Yes

No

Would your use of the image be an infringement of the copyright?

No

Yes

Can you assert fair use as a defense to the infringement?

Yes

No

Do you have any other defenses to the infringement?

Yes

No

USE THE IMAGE

DON'T USE THE IMAGE

Quotations and Compilations

intend to publish postcards with quotations about different subjects by famous people. I see that many websites with collections of quotations have copyright notices at the end of the sites. It is the same with books of quotations. How can you copyright a quotation by Picasso, Renoir or Goethe?

COPYRIGHT
(COMPILATIONS)

COPYRIGHT
(ORIGINALITY
REQUIREMENT)

PUBLIC DOMAIN

INFRINGEMENT

FEIST
PUBLICATIONS V.
RURAL TELEPHONE
SERVICE CO., INC.

Are quotations protected by copyright?

Let's review our copyright basics. First, we know that copyright does not protect names, titles or short phrases (http://www.copyright.gov/circs/circ34.pdf). If the quotation is a short phrase, it's probably not copyrightable at all.

Assuming the quotation is copyrightable, however, recall the other requirements for copyright protection: the work must be original and fixed in a tangible medium of expression (see Figure 1). If the person to whom the quotation is attributed never fixed the quotation in a tangible medium of expression, the quotation is not protected by copyright. And if someone else fixed the quotation in a tangible medium it's still not protected. Why? Because in such case the quotation would not be original to that person.

What if the quotation is copyrightable and it was fixed in a tangible medium of expression by its original author? Then we do some math (see Conversation #21) and determine whether the quotation has passed into the public domain. If the alleged work was **published** before 1923 it is in the public domain. That pretty much clears quotations attributable to Pierre-August Renoir, who died in 1919 and Johann Wolfgang von Goethe, who died in 1832. Pablo Picasso, however, died in 1973. Theoretically, then, a work by Picasso – whether a painting or a copyrightable quotation – could still be subject to copyright protection.

If you suspect the quotation you wish to use might be protected by copyright and has not passed into the public domain, you must obtain permission to use it, either from the author him/herself or from that person's estate.

The sites and books Reader describes are **compilations** of quotations. Under the Copyright Act a compilation is "*a work formed by the collective assembling of preexisting materials or of data that are selected, coordinated or arranged in such a way that the resulting work as a whole constitutes an original work of authorship*" (17 USC §101). The copyright notices Reader observes probably don't cover the quotations themselves, but rather the compilers' selection, arrangement and coordination of the quotations. As long as the compilers' editorial decisions reflect a threshold amount of creativity and judgment, the compilation (i.e., the book or the website) qualifies for copyright protection (*Feist Publications v. Rural Telephone Service Co., Inc.* 499 US 340 [1991]).

Compilers receive protection only for their editorial contributions in creating a compilation – not for the substantive material compiled. If a quotation is not copyrightable or has passed into the public domain, therefore, it remains "free for the taking" notwithstanding issuance of copyright protection for any compilation in which it happens to appear.

Owning the Piece (as opposed to) Owning the Copyright

a corporation wants to buy one of my art pieces and also use the image on brochures, catalogs, flyers, etc. for an upcoming convention. I'm not sure how to handle this and I don't know if these are two separate transactions. Can they use the image just because they own the artwork, or do they need my permission? Am I entitled to a separate fee? Should I have a contract?

LICENSES
(EXCLUSIVE AND
NONEXCLUSIVE)

ASSIGNMENTS

VIACOM
INTERNATIONAL V.
FANZINE
INTERNATIONAL

First of all: of course you should have a contract. You should always have a contract, and it should always be in writing. Period.

And yes, these are two separate transactions. Remember, copyright is a "bundle" of rights (see Conversation #4). Distinct components of the bundle include, for example, the right to reproduce the work, to distribute the work, to perform the work, to display the work publicly and to create derivative works based upon the work (see Figure 1).

When a buyer purchases your work, the buyer acquires the piece. The buyer does not acquire your copyright in the piece, nor any of the individual components of your copyright bundle. Those, you keep (17 USC §202). Within limits the buyer can do whatever she wishes with the piece (see Conversation #18), but unless you formally transfer your copyright interest, in writing, she acquires no copyright interest in the work. In order to acquire any copyright interest, the purchaser must obtain from you (in addition to the piece itself) either a **license** or a written **assignment**.

An "assignment," which must be in writing, transfers your entire copyright interest, i.e., each individual component of the bundle, to another party. After you execute an assignment, you no longer own any copyright interest in the work.

A "license" transfers just one or more – but not all – components from the copyright bundle. A license can be "exclusive," meaning that once you have granted it to one party, you cannot grant the same right to anyone else. **Exclusive licenses** must be in writing. A license can also be "nonexclusive." In that case, you can grant the same right over and over, to as many parties as you wish. **Nonexclusive licenses** do not need to be in writing.

Let's return to Reader's fact pattern.

The corporation purchases one piece of Reader's work. The corporation acquires the piece, and nothing else. The Copyright Act provides:

> Ownership of a copyright, or of any of the exclusive rights under a copyright, is distinct from ownership of any material object in which the work is embodied. Transfer of ownership of any material object, including the copy or phonorecord in which the work is first fixed, does not of itself convey any rights in the copyrighted work embodied in the object; nor, in the absence of an agreement, does transfer of ownership of a copyright or of any exclusive rights under a copyright convey property rights in any material object.

17 USC §202

Now the corporation wishes to reproduce copies of the piece on their convention brochure. That's an entirely separate transaction, and one for which Reader should be separately compensated. The right to reproduce the work is a component of Reader's exclusive bundle of copyright rights (see Figure 1). Even though the corporation owns the piece, it will be committing copyright infringement if it exercises any component of Reader's copyright bundle without a license. If the corporation wishes to reproduce copies of the work, therefore, it must first acquire a license from Reader to do so.

When this issue is **litigated**, the infringing party usually argues they had a license to exercise one or more of the bundle of rights with respect to the material object they obtained from the artist or copyright owner. Such was the case in *Viacom Int'l, Inc.* v. *Fanzine Int'l, Inc.* (2000 U.S. Dist. LEXIS 19960, S.D.N.Y., 2000). In *Viacom*, defendant Fanzine hired a graphic designer to create two commercial products, each containing exact reproductions of characters from television programs appearing on Nickelodeon, which is owned and operated by Viacom. Fanzine's designer telephoned Nickelodeon's publicity department merely to inquire about the procedure for obtaining photographic material. He did not request any specific material, nor did he request a license to use any specific material. The next day, however, the designer received a package of material from Nickelodeon, including 1" by 1.5" slides with the art in question. Without any further discussion, Fanzine used the slides to reproduce the character images on its products. Viacom then sued for copyright infringement, and won.

When their designer received the slides, Fanzine obtained… what? Single pieces of copyrighted works of art. Fanzine did not acquire any copyright interest in those individual pieces. Thus, when Fanzine reproduced those works without a license from Viacom, Fanzine committed copyright infringement. Fanzine argued that by sending the material Nickelodeon (Viacom) granted Fanzine an implied license to use the slides. The court disagreed, stating:

> Copyright law places on a putative licensee the burden of showing an agreement allowing it to reproduce protected material: the mere transfer of an object (such as the slides) in which copyrighted material is embodied does not imply a license to engage in copying of that object. See 17 U.S.C. § 202. If there is ambiguity concerning the rights conveyed when a copyright owner transfers such an object, such ambiguities are resolved in favor of finding a transfer of only the material object, not rights in the copyrighted work. See Shugrue v. Continental Airlines, Inc., 977 F. Supp. 280, 285 (S.D.N.Y. 1997).

> Even though the corporation owns the piece, it will be committing copyright infringement if it exercises any component of Reader's copyright bundle without a license. If the corporation wishes to reproduce copies of the work, therefore, it must first acquire a license from Reader to do so.

Joint Authorship and Work Made for Hire

h ere's a weird thing. If you happen to create copyrightable material in the course of your employment for someone else, your employer is the **author**, even though you did all the work.

At least initially, the "author" of a work owns its copyright. And that's a valuable thing, because whoever owns the copyright has the right to make money from the work – and to prevent others from doing so.

Not surprisingly, therefore, an enormous body of case law has arisen from disputes over copyright ownership. Two of the concepts central to such disputes are joint authorship and work made for hire.

Joint Authorship. There are three requirements for joint authorship. First, all purported authors must intend to be joint authors at the time they make their contributions to the work. There needs to be evidence of such prior intent among all joint authors, at the time they make their contributions to the work, in order to prove joint authorship. You can't just claim joint authorship after-the-fact, when the work starts to make money. If you do intend to share authorship with someone else, best practice is to have a written agreement to that effect, before either of you contributes anything to the work.

You need to have intent not only that all contributors will be joint authors, but that the contributions of all joint authors will be merged with the contributions of all other joint authors to create a single, unitary work.

Finally, in order to establish joint authorship you need to show that each joint author contributed material that was, itself, separately copyrightable.

I'm not an artist, but I'll use myself as an example. Even though my copyrighted material is writing, the following concepts apply equally to visual art.

I am the author of this book and I own all copyright rights to it. Let's just say, for fun, that before sitting down to write I had a chat with my neighbor, Kevin, about my outline for the book. Kevin had some great ideas, which I used. Then let's say…for fun…that this book went on to garner kudos beyond my wildest dreams and generated such demand that reprint rights alone afforded me the prospect of a luxurious retirement on the French Riviera. (I may not be an artist, but I have a good imagination!) Life was good indeed, until Kevin showed up claiming that he was a joint author of the book, and thus entitled to one-half of my riches.

Is Kevin a joint author of the book?

Mercifully for my retirement, he is not.

Ideas are not copyrightable so Kevin's claim of joint authorship fails on this point. Recall from Conversation #6, too, that in order to acquire copyright protection, expression must be reduced to a "fixed form." Further, even if Kevin's alleged contribution had been separately copyrightable, there is no evidence that – at the time of our conversation – we both intended to share in authorship of the book.

Work Made For Hire. If your copyrightable material is "work made for hire"

(WMFH), someone else is the legal author of the work. There are two ways this can happen. The first is if you are a true "employee" and you create the work within the scope of your employment. If, for example, you are a graphic artist employed by an advertising agency, copyright to the material you create belongs to your employer and not to you.

Disputes often arise over whether an employer-employee relationship actually exists. The leading case on this point is *Community for Creative Non-Violence* v. *Reid* (490 US 730 [1989]). In *Reid* the United States Supreme Court set forth a long list of factors that figure into determining whether someone is an employee or an independent contractor (see Figure 3). No single factor is determinative, and all situations are decided ultimately on a case-by-case basis.

FIGURE 3

FACTORS TO CONSIDER IN DETERMINING WHETHER AN INDIVIDUAL IS AN EMPLOYEE OR AN INDEPENDENT CONTRACTOR

(*Community for Creative Non-Violence* v. *Reid*, 490 US 730 [1989])

The hiring party's right to control the manner and means by which the product is accomplished

The skill required to do the work

The source of instrumentalities and tools used by the hired party

Location: where the hired party performs the work

The duration of the relationship between the parties

Whether the hiring party has the right to assign additional projects to the hired party

The extent of the hired party's discretion over when and how long to work

The method of payment

The hired party's role in hiring and paying assistants

Whether the work is part of the regular business of the hiring party

Whether the hiring party is in business at all

The provision of employee benefits to the hired party

The tax treatment of the hired party

No single factor is determinative!

If there is no employment relationship, work is WMFH only if it was specially ordered or commissioned, and there is a written agreement to that effect signed by both parties, and the work falls within one of the following nine special categories:

- contributions to a collective work (e.g., a magazine, anthology, encyclopedia, etc.);

- contributions to a motion picture or other audiovisual work;

- translations;

- supplementary works (e.g., introductions, forewords, illustrations, maps, charts, tables, editorial notes, musical arrangements, bibliographies, appendices, indexes etc.);

- compilations (i.e., a work formed by the collection and assembly of pre-existing material);
- instructional texts;
- tests;
- answer material for tests; or
- an atlas

17 USC §101

If someone other than your employer commissions you to create a work of art and the work does not fall into one of those nine categories, the work cannot be WMFH. Period. Even if there's a written contract saying it's a work for hire, it's not. If the commissioning party wants to obtain copyright rights to the work and you agree (and bargain for appropriate compensation!) you, the author, must specifically transfer the copyright rights in a separate written **assignment** (see Conversation #9).

Back in the day, Congress tried to add "photographic or other portraits" to §101's list of works eligible for WMFH status. The Register of Copyrights successfully blocked this attempt, stating:

Artists and photographers are among the most vulnerable and poorly protected of all the beneficiaries of the copyright law, and it seems clear that, like serious composers and choreographers, they were not intended to be treated as 'employees' under the carefully negotiated definition [of WMFH] in section 101.

Community for Creative Non-Violence v. Reid, 490 US 730, 747 n 13

> **If someone other than your employer commissions you to create a work of art and the work does not fall into one of those nine categories, the work cannot be WMFH. Period.**

The work made for hire doctrine is a complicated concept that shall occupy our attention in subsequent conversations. In the meantime, the following two points are key:

- If you're not an employee and your work isn't in one of the nine categories under §101 it's not WMFH, no matter what anybody tries to tell you; and
- If it is in one of the nine categories, it's only WMFH if you and the commissioning party have a signed, written agreement to that effect.

Developments in the Work Made for Hire Doctrine

n October 2003 the United States District Court for the District of Rhode Island issued a significant "work made for hire" (WMFH) decision involving a staff photographer at Brown University (*Foraste* v. *Brown University*, 290 F Supp 2d 234, D.R.I. 2003). This conversation will review the basic concepts of WMFH, and will examine how the court applied those concepts in *Foraste*. (Although we discuss WMFH concepts in other conversations, repeating them here is essential for understanding *Foraste*. The repetition is intentional, and a little review won't kill you.)

FORASTE V. BROWN UNIVERSITY

BUNDLE OF RIGHTS

WORK MADE FOR HIRE DOCTRINE

COPYRIGHT ASSIGNMENT AND TRANSFERABILITY

Basic Concepts. Anyone who creates copyrightable material is called the "author" of that material. The author of the work owns all copyright interests in the work and thus controls the "bundle of rights" that goes along with copyright ownership (see Figure 1). That "bundle" includes the following exclusive rights:

- to reproduce the work;

- to prepare derivative works based upon the copyrighted material;

- to distribute copies of the work to the public, whether by sale, rental, lease or lending;

- to perform the copyrighted work publicly;

- to display the copyrighted work publicly; and

- in the case of sound recordings, to perform the copyrighted work publicly by means of a digital audio transmission

17 USC §106

WMFH represents an exception to the general rule of copyright ownership. The creator does not own the copyright to work that qualifies as WMFH.

17 USC **§201(b)** provides:

In the case of a work made for hire, the employer or other person for whom the work was prepared is considered the author for purposes of [the Copyright Act] and, unless the parties have expressly agreed otherwise in a written instrument signed by them, owns all of the rights comprised in the copyright

Work qualifies as WMFH in one of two ways. If you create work in the course of an employer-employee relationship, your employer is considered the author of the work and the employer owns and controls the bundle of exclusive copyright rights (17 USC §§101, 201[b]).

Outside of an employment situation, you can also agree with another party to treat certain work as WMFH, but only if there is a written agreement to that effect signed by both parties, and only if the work falls within one of the nine special categories we discussed in Conversation #10: contributions to a collective work (e.g., a magazine, anthology, encyclopedia, etc.); contributions to a motion picture or other audiovisual work; translations; supplementary works (e.g., introductions, forewords, illustrations, maps, charts, tables, editorial notes, musical arrangements, bibliographies, appendices, indices, etc.); compilations (i.e., work formed by the collection and assembly of pre-existing material); instructional texts; tests; answer material for tests; or atlases.

If your work doesn't fall into one of the nine categories and it was not created in the course of employment, the work is not WMFH and can never be WMFH, even if you sign an agreement saying it is. People use this phrase very loosely, often not realizing that work can only be WMFH under the limited circumstances described above. Don't make the same mistake.

If you are the employer, and you truly wish to waive your WMFH rights, you need to do so in a written instrument signed by you and each individual employee.

If you and another party agree that the other party should own and control the bundle of rights to your work, but the work cannot be WMFH, you must affirmatively transfer the bundle of rights to the other party. (Sometimes you will hear the term **assignment** in connection with transferring rights. The words are essentially synonyms, as an "assignment" is a permanent transfer; see Conversations #4 and #9).

Though "intellectual property," copyright interests are transferred to other parties in the same manner as **personal property** (i.e. stuff).

17 USC **§201(d)** provides:

*The ownership of a copyright may be transferred in whole or in part by any means of conveyance or by operation of law, and may be bequeathed by will or pass as personal property by the applicable laws of **intestate succession**.*

In plain English: you can transfer or dispose of your copyright interests (that is, any one or more of the rights from the "bundle") just as you would transfer or dispose of your car or your diamond ring or any of your other "stuff."

If you transfer your copyright and the transfer is not by **operation of law**, the transfer must be in writing and signed by you.

17 USC **§204(a)** provides:

A transfer of copyright ownership, other than by operation of law, is not valid unless an instrument of conveyance, or a note or memorandum of the transfer, is in writing and signed by the owner of the rights conveyed or such owner's duly authorized agent.

Foraste v. *Brown University*

John Foraste was a full-time photographer employed by Brown University (Brown) between 1975 and 1998. Brown was Mr. Foraste's employer and Mr. Foraste took photographs for Brown in the regular course of his employment. There is no question that the photographs Mr. Foraste took for Brown were WMFH, making Brown the legal "author" of such photographs.

In 1986 Brown adopted the following policy:

It is the University's position that, as a general premise, ownership of copyrightable property which results from performance of one's University duties and activities will belong to the author or originator. This applies to books, art works, software, etc.

Quiz (and be honest): Do you think the Policy changed anything? Were Mr. Foraste's photographs still considered WMFH or, after the Policy, did copyright revert to Mr. Foraste?

We know that Mr. Foraste's work was, in the first instance, WMFH. So at least initially, Brown held the copyright rights. However, Mr. Foraste alleged that through the Policy Brown transferred its copyright interests in the photographs back to him. Upon that theory, he sued Brown for copyright infringement.

Take a look at sections 201(b) and 201(d) of the Copyright Act, set forth above. Mr. Foraste argued that section **201(d)** allows an owner to transfer copyright by any means of conveyance, and thus the Policy was sufficient to transfer the photograph rights from Brown (the acknowledged WMFH owner) to him. Brown, however, contended that section **201(b)** creates an exception for WMFH requiring, for the transfer of rights to such work, a written instrument signed both by the creator and the employer or current owner of the rights.

Certainly, Brown's argument ran counter to the spirit of its own policy. But legally the argument prevailed. The court held that section 201(b) was intended to protect employers' interests and thus required a writing and signatures on any agreement altering the WMFH ownership scheme. Because neither Brown nor Mr. Foraste had signed it, the Policy did not comply with section 201(b); therefore Brown had not effectively transferred its ownership interests in the photographs to Mr. Foraste.

Brown won this case, based on the court's interpretation of section 201(b). However, the court went on to address "what if." What if Mr. Foraste had been correct, and a transfer could occur under section 201(d)? Even if that were possible, the court determined, the transfer would still be subject to section **204(a)** – which also requires a written signature from the party transferring its rights. The court analyzed a long line of cases interpreting section 204(a), and found that the Policy failed as a section 204(a) transfer instrument.

> If you are the employee and you want to retain your copyright ownership rights, do not rely on an institutional policy like Brown's. Insist on an individualized written instrument, signed by you and the employer

Bottom line: WMFH is WMFH, and even if employers have policies supposedly "waiving" their copyright ownership rights, such policies might not be effective. If you are the employer, and you truly wish to waive your WMFH rights, you need to do so in a written instrument signed by you and each individual employee. If you are the employee and you want to retain your copyright ownership rights, do not rely on an institutional policy like Brown's. Insist on an individualized written instrument, signed by you and the employer.

Batman v. The Artist: Copyright's "Architectural Exception"

riddler? Joker? Penguin? They never stand a chance! Batman does not lose. Even in court, victory belongs to the Caped Crusader. His courtroom nemesis: The Artist.

This conversation looks at copyright protection (or lack thereof) for sculptural works that are permanent, integral components of buildings. *Leicester* v. *Warner Brothers* (232 F3d 1212, 9th Cir 2000) is a leading case on point. In that matter a sculptor (The Artist) worked side-by-side with an architect to incorporate sculptural elements into the design of a building. Warner Brothers filmed the building – without The Artist's permission – and used it as the "Second Bank of Gotham" in the movie, *Batman Forever*. The Artist sued Warner Brothers (Batman) for copyright infringement and of course...lost.

Before diving into this conversation let's review some basic concepts (see Conversations #4 and #6). Among other things, copyright protects pictorial, graphic and sculptural (PGS) work. Copyright does not protect "useful articles," which, under the law, are defined as: *"[articles] having an intrinsic utilitarian function that is not merely to portray the appearance of the article or to convey information"* (17 USC §101).

We all know that art can be a component of useful articles. Jewelry, for example, is as much artistic expression as it is functional and useful. Sculpture can be useful too, as, for example, when it serves as the base of a lamp. Does such art lose its copyright protection simply because it is also functional? No. Copyright protection is available for PGS work if (and here is the test) it has "features that can be identified separately from, and are capable of existing independently of, the utilitarian aspects of the article." Basically, if the art can stand on its own as pure art and the useful article can still function without it, the art is eligible for copyright protection (see Copyright Office Factsheet FL-103, http://www.copyright.gov/fls/fl103.pdf).

Until 1990 buildings were "useful articles" and, once built, they were ineligible for copyright protection. The architect's plans were protectible as PGS work, but the buildings themselves were not. In 1990 Congress passed the Architectural Works Copyright Protection Act (AWCPA) and buildings became eligible for copyright protection (see Copyright Office Circular 41, http://www.copyright.gov/circs/circ41.pdf).

Buildings did not, however, acquire the full bundle of copyright rights that PGS works enjoy (see Figure 1). The AWCPA carved out a major exception for architectural works known, astonishingly, as, "the architectural exception." The architectural exception provides that, even though buildings have copyright protection, it's still OK (and not an infringement) for someone to make a "pictorial representation" of the building as long as the building is ordinarily visible from a public place (17 USC §120). In other words, you can paint a picture of the building, you can photograph the building, you can film it and you can make any other kind of "pictorial representation" without infringing the building's copyright. The architectural exception also states that in addition to making your pictorial representation

you can distribute it and/or display it in a public place. You can't do any of those things with copyrighted PGS work.

This is all very cool if you're an artist or a tourist and the building is your subject. It's not so wonderful if you're the copyright holder on the building or a sculptor who shares in the building's copyright.

Why would a sculptor share in the building's copyright? Joint authorship. When two or more people collaborate on a work and each contributes material that, itself, would be separately eligible for copyright protection, the collaborators are "joint authors" (17 USC §201[a]; see Conversation #10). Unless there is a written agreement to the contrary, each joint author owns an equal share to the copyright of the work as a whole. In the Batman case, The Artist (the sculptor) and the architect were joint authors of the building.

Back to Gotham. The Artist said to Batman (Warner Brothers): "Sculpture is PGS work, not subject to the architectural exception. If you want to film my sculpture, pay me!" Warner Brothers refused, so The Artist sued for copyright infringement. Here's what happened.

As his contribution to the building, The Artist designed artistic elements of a courtyard, towers and a street wall to convey an allegorical history of the City of Los Angeles and its vampire-like relationship with water. Warner Brothers' first legal hurdle was to establish that The Artist's work was "integrated" and "part of the design plan" of the building. The court found that it was.

Next, the court had to determine whether, as an integral part of the building, The Artist's work was subject to the architectural exception – just like the building itself. If so, The Artist's work would lose a big chunk of its copyright protection and would be "fair game" for people to make and display pictorial representations, at will.

Warner Brothers, of course, argued that The Artist's sculpture, as an integral part of the building, was subject to the architectural exception. The Artist, on the other hand, argued that even if sculptural work is "integrated" into the design of the building, artists still have the right to protect such work separately, as PGS material. The court agreed with Batman. Finding for Warner Brothers, the court determined that once sculptural work is integrated into the design of a building, it loses full PGS copyright protection and is subject to the architectural exception. Said the court, "it would be counterintuitive to suppose that Congress (in the AWCPA) meant to restrict pictorial copying to some, but not all of, a unitary architectural work" (*Leicester* v. *Warner Brothers* (232 F3d at 1220).

> ...the court determined that once sculptural work is integrated into the design of a building, it loses full PGS copyright protection and is subject to the architectural exception.

And you have to admit, if The Artist's argument had prevailed it would be nearly impossible for the general public to know which part of a building was "fair game" because of the architectural exception and which part was "off-limits" due to a sculptor's PGS copyright.

Batman thus vanquished The Artist. Remember, though, that "Batman" also represents the interests of artists who, like Warner Brothers, wish to use a building as the subject of their own work. I would imagine that many Readers side with Batman in this case, notwithstanding understandable sympathies toward their colleague, The Artist.

There's a lesson, too, if you're The Artist. If you are creating art that's going to become an integral part of a building, remember to negotiate a higher fee in anticipation of your work becoming subject to the architectural exception and its lesser measure of copyright protection.

Legal Self-Help:
Why Contracts Are Like Dentures

need to obtain written permission to use a photographer's image in my paint-
ing. What do I say when I ask? Should there be some sort of contract? If so,
where can I find one?

Thanks, Reader. Those are great questions.

Rule number one. We don't "find" contracts. We draft them, or we have them drafted for us, on a transaction-by-transaction basis. When readers ask me to recommend sources for forms and "sample" contracts, I always refuse. No two transactions will ever be the same; thus no "sample" form will ever provide adequate protection for you or the person with whom you are doing business.

Rule number two. You get what you pay for. Would you buy your dentures off the shelf at Dentu-Mart? Of course not. Why? Because unless your dentures are crafted specifically for you, they're going to hurt like heck, you'll drool a lot and sooner or later you'll end up spending money anyway, to get teeth that actually work. Just like dentures, contracts must be crafted specifically for you.

Enough said. Let's turn to Reader's primary concern: requesting permission to use someone else's work. The paragraphs that follow address just a few of the many issues one must consider when clearing the rights to copyrighted material. As you read these paragraphs, think about whether you'd be comfortable handling the transaction with a "canned" form.

It's a Contract. Obtaining permission is a contractual transaction between you (Artist) and the person (Owner) who owns rights to the material you want to use. Formation of a contract requires a valid **offer**, a valid **acceptance**, and legal **consideration**. You make the offer when you ask for permission (e.g., "In exchange for X, will you grant me permission to use your material?") If Owner agrees to the terms of your offer, Owner "accepts." You are then required to provide something of value to Owner (e.g., money, or your promise to use the material only within the scope of permission granted), and Owner is required to provide something of value to you (e.g., the permission, or Owner's promise not to sue when you use the material). What each of you provides to the other is called, "consideration." Once you've got all three elements – offer, acceptance and consideration – you've got a legally enforceable contract.

Get it in Writing. Reader says she needs "written permission" to use the photographer's image. Must a contract always be in writing? No. Should a contract always be in writing? Absolutely. As a wise woman once said, "an oral contract isn't worth the paper it's written on." (Actually, that quote is widely attributed to movie mogul Samuel Goldwyn, and this is my contribution to the distortion of urban legend.) Whatever. Get it in writing.

License or Release? Do you need a license or a release, or both? Do you know the difference? A **license** is an affirmative grant of rights; e.g., Artist may create, publish and distribute a single derivative work based on Owner's photograph but may not exercise any of Owner's other copyright rights in the photograph. A **release** is a promise not to sue; e.g., Artist may use Person's image in Artist's work and Person will not sue Artist for violating Person's **right of privacy** or **right of publicity**.

What rights do you need? Remember, copyright is a "bundle" of six distinct rights (see Figure 1). Owner can license all or part of that bundle. You must understand and articulate in your agreement, which parts of the "bundle" you need.

Exclusive or nonexclusive? Do you need an "exclusive" license or a "nonexclusive" license? If Owner grants certain rights to Artist in an **exclusive** license, Owner may not turn around and grant those same rights to anyone else, at any time during the Term of the license. On the other hand, if Owner grants only a **nonexclusive** license, Owner could grant those same rights to every artist on Earth, at will. (Speaking of the "Term" of the license: For how long do you need the license? When will it expire? Why is "Term" capitalized?)

Does Owner really own the rights you seek? Suppose Artist and Owner enter into a contract whereby Owner grants Artist a license to use Owner's photograph in her (Artist's) painting. That license wouldn't be worth a darn to Artist if, for example, Owner had taken the photo as a work made for hire; nor if he had sold (or "assigned" or "transferred") his copyright interests in the photo to someone else; nor if he had already granted an exclusive license to another party. In any of those scenarios, the license is worthless because Owner had no authority to grant it in the first place. How does Artist protect herself against such a result?

Does anyone else have rights to images that appear in the photograph? Just because you obtain rights from Owner doesn't mean that others don't also have rights you'll need to clear (see Conversation #4). Do you need a model release? A property release? A trademark license? Does your "canned" contract address these issues?

Are you and Owner both competent to contract? What is the age of majority in your state? In Owner's state? Why does it matter?

Do you really need permission? Is the material you want to use in the **public domain**? If the material is not in the public domain, you need a license. But if it is, you don't need permission at all. You can copy it; you can sell it (if anyone will buy); you can display it; you can create derivative works based upon it; etc. Do you know how to tell whether material is or is not in the public domain (Conversation #21)?

> **Formation of a contract requires a valid offer, a valid acceptance, and legal consideration.**

Here's a common myth:

> *If I don't sell my product or make any money from it, I don't need permission to use someone else's work in my own.*

Whether you sell your work (or not) is irrelevant. The minute you use or incorporate Owner's copyrighted work into your own, you infringe upon Owner's copyright, unless either a.) you have a license to use the work, or b.) your use is protected under a statutory exception such as the **fair use** doctrine (see Conversation #7). Do you know how to make a fair use determination? Do you know about other defenses and exceptions?

Will Owner acquire any copyright interest(s) in your work? It could happen, if you don't fully understand the contract. Can you analyze a contract well enough to protect yourself?

What if you die? What if Owner dies? Will the license remain in effect? If not, what happens?

Suppose you have a dispute? Will you go to arbitration, or straight to court? Which state's laws will apply?

Does all this really matter? You bet. Just like Dentu-Mart dentures, canned legal forms are incapable of serving your needs adequately in all circumstances. Correcting your mistakes will almost always be more expensive than drafting your contract properly in the first place.

"But I can't afford a lawyer!"

I know. Really, I do. Lawyers cost money; times are tough; you've got six kids at Harvard. All legitimate concerns. But I still won't recommend any form contracts.

(Please note, I have no pecuniary motivation for taking this position. To the contrary, a substantial portion of my income derives from helping artists clean up messes they could have prevented in the first place, had they invested in legal counsel.)

Instead, let's look at some reasonable alternatives to self-help. Many states have "volunteer lawyers for the arts" (VLA) organizations. Some are simple projects of the local bar association; others are well-established entities unto themselves. If you can't afford a lawyer, check to see if there's a VLA group that serves your region. New York Volunteer Lawyers for the Arts has a great website that includes, among other resources, a listing of VLA groups nationwide: http://www.vlany.org/res_dir.html

> If you strike out with the bar association and cannot find an attorney to help you on a pro bono or reduced-fee basis, do something you're already good at: think creatively.

If you can't find an arts-specific legal services organization, consult your state and local bar associations and ask generally about their *pro bono* programs. You can find contact information for practically any bar association, worldwide, at the Hieros Gamos website: http://www.hg.org/bar.html

If you strike out with the bar association and cannot find an attorney to help you on a *pro bono* or reduced-fee basis, do something you're already good at: think creatively. Is there a law school nearby? Check to see if the law school has a legal services clinic for which you might qualify. Law students entrusted with real cases are highly motivated to do a good job. Unlike working attorneys, they're unburdened by heavy caseloads (which means more time to spend with you) and eager to show potential employers that they have real world experience. If the law school doesn't maintain a clinic for which you qualify, organize a group of colleagues and make a presentation asking the law school to create such a clinic.

If self-help is the only option, study hard. Nolo (http://www.nolo.com) and Allworth Press (http://www.allworth.com) specialize in self-help publications. New York VLA also has a list of books and publications on its website: http://www.vlany.org/res_lib.html

All Rights Reserved:
International Copyright Treaties

a ll Rights Reserved." We've all seen it after copyright notices, for example: "Copyright © 2005 Marybeth Peters. All Rights Reserved." We've seen it, yes. But we don't see it all the time. So what does it mean, and when is it necessary?

BUENOS AIRES CONVENTION

By and large, "All Rights Reserved" is a holdover from days gone by, with little remaining significance. Here's the story.

BERNE CONVENTION

COPYRIGHT NOTICE

Copyright protection is not international. That is to say, if you obtain a copyright in the United States your work is not automatically protected in, for example, Nepal. Protection in a foreign country depends upon the law(s) of that country.

Does that mean you have to study the copyright laws of every single country in order to know your rights? Yes and no. Although the law of the country still controls, a number of international copyright treaties (called **conventions**) simplify the daunting prospect of sifting through foreign statutes.

The Berne Convention eliminated the requirement of affixing notice to a work in order to obtain copyright protection. That is why, in the United States and other Berne countries, placing a copyright notice on your work is now optional.

There are two main international copyright treaties: The Berne Convention and the Universal Copyright Convention. If a particular country is a party (also called a **signatory**) to one or both conventions, you can predict with a certain degree of confidence what the copyright laws of that country might be. That's because the treaties set forth certain standards, and in order to be a party to the treaty, the signatory country must substantially adopt those standards as its own. (The United States joined the Universal Copyright Convention in 1955, and the Berne Convention in 1989.)

"Fascinating," you muse, "but what does this have to do with All Rights Reserved?"

Thanks for asking.

Once upon a time, there was an international copyright treaty known as the Buenos Aires Convention of 1911. (And in case you're ever on a quiz show, you might want to know that President Woodrow Wilson officially proclaimed the United States' adherence to the Buenos Aires Convention on July 13, 1914.)

Besides the United States, most signatories to the Buenos Aires Convention were Latin American countries. The Convention provided that work copyrighted in one signatory country received protection in all other signatory countries without the necessity of registration in the other countries. The catch, however, was that the work did need to contain a notice reserving these rights, and the most common phrase used for this purpose was...you guessed it...All Rights Reserved.

As time marched on, bigger and better treaties pushed the Buenos Aires Convention into obscurity. The Berne Convention eliminated the requirement of affixing notice to a work in order to obtain copyright protection. That is why, in the United

States and other Berne countries, placing a copyright **notice** on your work is now optional. Most Buenos Aires signatories eventually joined the Berne Convention, thus in most countries "All Rights Reserved" is no longer necessary.

The Copyright Office's Circular 38a has information on most of the major international copyright treaties. It also offers an alphabetical list of nations and the treaties to which each is a signatory: http://www.copyright.gov/circs/circ38a.pdf

Quiz:

1.) Why, above, did I choose Nepal as an example; and

2.) Who is Marybeth Peters?

You'll find both answers online at the Copyright Office website.

Copyright Damages:
The Importance of Registration

Let's talk football.

This is the story of Frederick Bouchat, a Maryland security guard and amateur artist. When the Cleveland Browns football team announced its move to a new city (Baltimore) and adoption of a new identity (the Ravens), Mr. Bouchat took it upon himself to sketch some new logo designs for the team. He faxed one of his designs (the "Winged Shield" design) to the Chairman of the Maryland Stadium Authority, along with a note asking the Chairman to forward the design to the Ravens' president. Mr. Bouchat asked the Ravens to send him a letter of recognition and an autographed helmet if they used the Winged Shield design.

BOUCHAT V. BALTIMORE RAVENS, INC.

COPYRIGHT (STATUTORY DAMAGES)

SUMMARY JUDGMENT

COPYRIGHT (NOTICE AND REGISTRATION)

Guess what happened?

Of course, they used the design. (This wouldn't be a very exciting story, otherwise). But they didn't send a letter, and they didn't send a helmet. So Mr. Bouchat sued for copyright infringement, and won. (*Bouchat* v. *Baltimore Ravens, Inc.*, 215 F Supp 2d 611 [D. Md. 2002], affd 346 F3d 514 [4th Cir. 2003], cert denied ___US___, 124 S Ct. 2171, 158 L Ed 2d 732 [2004])

Sounds like a dream come true: a jury verdict – upheld on appeal – against the National Football League. Gotta be worth millions, right?

Herein lies the moral of this conversation: register your copyrights.

Not exactly, and herein lies the moral of this conversation: register your copyrights. Registration costs $30 and is relatively easy to accomplish (see Copyright Office Circular 40 http://www.copyright. gov/circs/circ40.pdf and Fact Sheet FL-115 http://www.copyright.gov/fls/ fl115.pdf). Had Mr. Bouchat registered the Winged Shield design with the Copyright Office prior to the infringement, he would have been eligible for potentially enormous **statutory damages**. But he hadn't registered, so he had to settle for the consolation prize: his own **actual damages** (of which there were none) and profits of the infringer that were "attributable to the infringement" (17 USC 504[b]).

Here's how the damages statute works. In order to measure an infringer's profits, the copyright owner needs only to present evidence of the infringer's gross revenue. Then it's up to the infringer to prove that its profits were attributable to factors other than the copyrighted work. (This is called "shifting the burden of proof.") Mr. Bouchat's lawyers contended that at least some portion of all Ravens revenue was attributable to the infringement, so the lawyers merely submitted evidence of the gross receipts from all Ravens activities (e.g., ticket sales, merchandise, royalties, etc.)

The Ravens made a motion for **summary judgment** arguing that Mr. Bouchat had cast too wide a net by claiming profits from all revenue sources. (*Stop. Go to the Glossary and look up summary judgment. It's important, in order to understand the rest of this story!*) The court agreed, and granted the Ravens' motion, restricting the available "pool" from which the jury could award damages. The court allowed revenue from t-shirts, caps, souvenir cups and a few other types of merchandise. Everything else (sponsorships, broadcasts, ticket sales, royalties and parking/concession revenue) was excluded from the pool. With apologies for mixing sports metaphors, this was "strike one" against Mr. Bouchat.

A damages trial proceeded, and the jury determined that the Ravens had submitted legally sufficient evidence that all profits – even from merchandise still in the "pool" – were attributable entirely to factors other than the Winged Shield design. Even though the Ravens had indisputably infringed, the jury awarded Mr. Bouchat absolutely nothing. Strike two.

His only remaining hope was reversal on appeal. Mr. Bouchat argued that the lower court had erred by excluding so many categories of merchandise from the "pool." His lawyers also contended that summary judgment in favor of an infringer – excluding portions of revenue from the damages pool – was not permissible. In October 2003 the Fourth Circuit Court of Appeals issued its decision, rejecting the appeal.

Strike three.

Once you get through the legal gobbledy-gook, the upshot of the Fourth Circuit's decision is that summary judgment in favor of an infringer, excluding certain sources of revenue, is permissible, but only if: a.) there is "no conceivable connection" between the infringement and those revenues, or b.) despite the existence of a conceivable connection, the copyright holder failed to offer evidence of a "causal link" between the infringement and the revenue.

Had Mr. Bouchat registered in time to qualify for statutory damages, he might have collected upwards of $150,000 per infringement. That's a lot of money. Instead, he walked away empty-handed, his victory painfully hollow.

Wait a minute. The copyright holder failed to offer evidence...? A few paragraphs ago we just said that the "burden of proof" had shifted to the infringer to show that their gross revenues were not attributable to the infringement. What gives?

That's what Mr. Bouchat wanted to know. In his view, he was entitled to the benefit of the presumption, under section 504 of the Copyright Act, that the infringer's revenues were entirely attributable to the infringement unless the infringer proved otherwise. Now all of a sudden it was he – the victim – who had to prove that the excluded categories actually were attributable to the infringement, just because the other side made a simple motion for summary judgment. Worse still, because summary judgment is a final determination made by a judge, he lost the opportunity to present his proof (regarding the excluded categories) to a jury. That didn't seem right to Mr. Bouchat.

The appeals court, however, had no problem with this approach so they set to analyzing the case under the "no conceivable connection" and "evidence of a causal link" tests. With respect to two categories of revenue (minimum guarantee shortfalls and free merchandise) the court found there was "no conceivable connection" between the Winged Shield and the revenue. Summary judgment excluding those two categories was therefore upheld.

With respect to the remaining excluded categories, the Fourth Circuit acknowledged that there could, conceivably, be a connection between the Winged Shield and the revenue. The next question, therefore, was: did Mr. Bouchat submit enough evidence to create a "question of fact" that profits from the excluded categories were attributable to the infringement? Please note, he didn't have to submit conclusive evidence at this point; to survive the summary judgment motion his lawyers only had to submit enough evidence to establish a "question of fact" for the jury.

Mr. Bouchat's lawyers submitted nothing at all. In response to the summary judgment motion they simply relied, once again, on their evidence establishing the total gross receipts generated by all Ravens activities. They didn't submit a single thing drawing a "causal link" between those revenues and the Winged Shield design. Mr. Bouchat thereupon flunked the "causal link" test, and summary judgment on the remaining excluded categories was upheld.

Frederick Bouchat's pool had officially run dry.

I recognize and apologize for the fact that this conversation is somewhat heavy on the legalese. In my view, though, it's important to present this tragic story in full detail, in order to convey the urgency of registering your copyrights in a timely manner. Had Mr. Bouchat registered in time to qualify for statutory damages, he might have collected upwards of $150,000 per infringement (see Conversation #16). That's a lot of money. Instead, he walked away empty-handed, his victory painfully hollow.

Before 1978, using the copyright notice and applying for **registration** was required in order to obtain copyright protection. Now, copyright attaches the moment you (the author) express the work in a fixed form. You don't have to use the notice and you don't have to register. As soon as you put pen to paper, brush to canvas, sound to recording…your work is copyrighted.

Most artists know this and many, unfortunately, see it as a time-saver: "I don't have to register, so why bother?"

The story of Frederick Bouchat should be answer enough.

CONVERSATION #16

Protecting Your Work
on the Internet

i am a self-taught photographer. I enjoy the traditional methods but realize the technological world is the place to become known and be seen. How does an artist protect his/her images on the internet? I am setting up a website and I want to display my work, but I also want to protect it from being taken by just anyone.

COPYRIGHT NOTICE

COPYRIGHT
REGISTRATION
(ONLINE WORK)

COPYRIGHT
REGISTRATION
(AUTOMATED
DATABASES)

COPYRIGHT
(STATUTORY
DAMAGES)

As a website operator you need to consider copyright from both sides of the table. In addition to protecting your own original work from **infringement**, you must also take measures to ensure that you do not infringe upon the work of others. A work does not lose its copyright protection simply because it appears online. Downloading someone else's copyrighted work without permission is infringement. Period. So make sure you have appropriate licenses to use all material that appears on your website. This means all text, music, video, designs, logos, etc. If you didn't create it yourself, get permission. (And remember, unless you received a written **assignment** of copyright, or the material is **work made for hire**, you don't own the copyright to work you paid someone else to create. They do.)

Protecting your own work is more difficult. Let's face it: there are no guarantees that someone won't download your work without permission. There are steps you can take, however, to prepare for the worst.

Downloading someone else's copyrighted work without permission is infringement.

First, place a copyright notice prominently on every page of your website, in your **metatags** and, if feasible, on or near the work itself. Copyright law no longer requires us to use the notice (see Conversation #14). Doing so, however, announces to the world that you are protecting your rights and, in the event of litigation, helps prevent an infringing party from advancing "innocent infringement" as a defense to **statutory damages** (17 USC §504[c]). Your notice should take the following form:

COPYRIGHT © [YEAR OF FIRST PUBLICATION] [YOUR NAME]

For more information about copyright notice, see Copyright Office Circular 3 at: http://www.copyright.gov/circs/circ03.pdf

Next, register your work with the United States Copyright Office. You have several options. Prior to placing material on the web, you could register each work that appears on the site, independently, using the appropriate registration form (i.e., Form VA for pictorial and graphic works; Form TX for literary material; Form SR for sound recordings, etc.) In certain situations you may register two or more works of visual art with a single application and a single fee (see Conversation #17 and Copyright Office Circular 40: http://www.copyright.gov/circs/circ40.pdf). In general, however, you must submit a separate application and a separate, nonrefundable $30 fee for each individual work of visual art.

Another option is to register the copyrightable elements of your website, together, as an "online work." (See Copyright Office Circular 66: http://www.copyright.gov/circs/circ66.pdf). You must be careful in the application to identify every copyrightable element on the site that you wish to protect. And if you've previously registered any element that appears on the site, you may not include such element in this application – you need to choose a single method of registration.

Notwithstanding an enormous body of online material, the Copyright Office still has no registration form specifically for online work. Accordingly, Circular 66 instructs us to "use the form that corresponds to the predominant material" on the site. If your site consists primarily of visual art, then, you'd use Form VA to register the website as an online work; if it consists primarily of text you'd use Form TX, etc.

What happens when you update the website? Does registration as an online work cover subsequent updates and revisions? No.[8] For that reason I instruct clients to re-register their sites on a regular basis.

Although registering your work with the Copyright Office is not required, it's always a good idea. For one thing, as they say, "infringement happens." If it happens to you, you can't bring an infringement action until you've registered the work in question (17 USC §411). So you might as well register now. Plus, if you've registered before infringement takes place, you might qualify for statutory damages. If not, you only qualify for "actual damages," or the actual amount of your loss (and the infringer's gain) as a result of the infringing activity. Typically, statutory damages are significantly greater than actual damages (see Conversation #15).

In a copyright infringement action the judge has discretion to award statutory damages to an eligible plaintiff "in a sum of not less than $750 nor more than $30,000" per infringement (17 USC §504[c][1]). If the infringement is found to be "willful," the court has discretion to award up to $150,000 per infringement (17 USC §504[c][2]). If, on the other hand, the infringer "was not aware and had no reason to believe that his or her acts constituted an infringement of copyright," the court may reduce statutory damages to not less than $200 per infringement (17 USC §504[c][2]). Whether you placed a notice on your work can be an important factor in determining whether infringing activity was "willful" or "innocent." And that determination can mean the difference between $200 per infringement or, potentially, $150,000.

> **Whether you placed a notice on your work can be an important factor in determining whether infringing activity was "willful" or "innocent." And that determination can mean the difference between $200 per infringement or, potentially, $150,000.**

In addition to taking legal precautions, there are technical measures you can take to protect your work online. For technical advice and a discussion of this issue from the artist's point of view, you may wish to consult *Electronic Highway Robbery: An Artist's Guide to Copyrights in the Digital Era* by Mary E. Carter [Peachpit Press, 1996]. (Note: Ms. Carter's book has not been updated. Still, however, it offers some very useful ideas for consideration.)

---

[8] Not unless your website is registered as an "automated database," in which case registration covers database revisions taking place within a three-month period. Most artists' sites are unlikely to qualify as automated databases. For further information consult Copyright Office Circular 65: http://www.copyright.gov/circs/circ65.pdf

Copyright Registration: Yes, There's More

Several years ago I sent 20 slides to the United States Copyright Office to be registered. I have made much new work since then. Do I have to keep sending slides of new work for the rest of my working life – or am I legally "covered" for all my work since that date forever?

From another Reader:

> *Does the $30 copyright registration fee cover all current and future pieces of my art – or do I have to register each piece?*

This conversation will discuss how much of your work can be "covered" by a single copyright registration.

Typically, a single application and fee ($30) covers a single work of authorship: that is, a single painting, a single book, a single song, etc. The Copyright Office's Circular 40 (Copyright Registration for Works of Visual Art) explains:

> *Registration covers only the particular work deposited for the registration. It does not give any sort of "blanket" protection to other works in the same series [nor] any earlier or later [work].*

Not only that, every time you revise the work, you need to re-register. Circular 40 states:

> *Each copyrightable version or issue must be registered to gain the advantages of registration for the new material it contains.*

Notwithstanding this general rule, in certain circumstances it is possible to register more than one work of visual art with a single application and fee. In order to do so, the works must be unpublished and properly assembled as a collection. You must satisfy all of the following conditions:

- The elements of the collection are assembled in an orderly form;

- The combined elements bear a single title identifying the collection as a whole;

- The copyright claimant or claimants for each element in the collection are the same; and

- All the elements are by the same author, or if they are by different authors, at least one author has contributed copyrightable authorship to each element.

As Circular 40 uses the term "element" it's referring to an individual "work." Thus, if you assembled an unpublished collection of paintings for registration, each individual painting would be an "element" of the collection.

The term "publication" also has a specialized definition in this context. As Circular 40 explains,

> *The copyright law defines "publication" as: the distribution of copies of a*

work to the public by sale or other transfer of ownership or by rental, lease, or lending. Offering to distribute copies to a group of persons for purposes of further distribution or public display also constitutes publication. A public display does not of itself constitute publication.

A work of art that exists in only one copy, such as a painting or statue, is not regarded as published when the single existing copy is sold or offered for sale in the traditional way, for example, through an art dealer, gallery, or auction house. A statue erected in a public place is not necessarily published.

In general, if your work remains unpublished and if you satisfy the other requirements for registering an unpublished collection (set forth in Circular 40), you may register more than one work with a single application and fee. A word of caution, however: works registered as an unpublished collection will be listed in the records of the Copyright Office only under the collection's title. Individual titles for the "elements" of the collection will not appear. Those individual elements still acquire copyright protection under the collective registration, but someone conducting a copyright search won't find any record of such protection. If it's important to you that a particular work be identified and searchable in the records of the Copyright Office, your best bet is to register that work separately.

Photographers may take advantage of another special provision, permitting group registrations for photographic work (Copyright Office Fact Sheet, FL-124, http://www.copyright.gov/fls/fl124.pdf):

A group of published photographs may be registered on a single form with a single fee if all the following conditions are met:

1. All the photographs are by the same photographer. If an employer for hire is named as author, only one photographer's work may be included; AND

2. All the photographs are published within the same calendar year; AND

3. All the photographs have the same copyright claimant(s)

There are some critical differences between this provision and Circular 40's "unpublished collection" provision. For one, FL-124 specifically applies to work that has been published within a single calendar year. Thus, to take advantage of this special photography provision, publication is actually required; whereas publication is a bar to using the "unpublished collection" provision for other works of visual art.

Both FL-124 and the "unpublished collection" provision refer to the copyright "claimant" and to the "author." Let's pause, because this can be confusing. The **author** is the person who actually created the work (or, if the work is **work made for hire**, the person deemed to have created the work), whether or not that person still owns the copyright. We've already established that at least initially, copyright in a work belongs to its author or authors (see Conversation #4). A copyright interest is an intellectual property asset, however, and as such, anyone owning the interest may transfer it to another person or entity. The **claimant** is the person who currently owns the copyright interest and is seeking to register that interest with the Copyright Office. The author of a work will always be its "author," but if he or she transfers ownership of the copyright interest, the author won't necessarily be the "claimant" when the work is registered.

> If it's important to you that a particular work be identified and searchable in the records of the Copyright Office, your best bet is to register that work separately.

Example. In the world of music publishing, songwriters routinely transfer their copyrights to publishing companies. The company, as legal owner of the copyright interest, then registers the song with the Copyright Office. For purposes of registering the song, the publishing company is the "claimant," while the song-writer remains the "author."

Back to photography and group registration. FL-124 contains a note of caution that merits thoughtful consideration:

> *If infringement of a published work begins before the work has been registered, the copyright owner can obtain the ordinary remedies for copyright infringement (including injunctions, actual damages and profits, and impounding and disposition of infringing articles). However, the owner cannot obtain special remedies (statutory damages and attorney's fees) unless registration was made before the infringement commenced or within 3 months after first publication of the work.*

If you choose to invoke FL-124 for photography your three-month grace period starts ticking from the date of publication for the earliest published photograph in the group.

∙∙∙∙∙∙∙∙∙∙∙∙∙∙∙∙∙∙∙∙∙∙∙∙∙∙∙∙∙∙∙∙

To be certain that your application, deposit, and fee are received in the Copyright Office within 3 months of publication of the earliest published photograph within the group, you may wish to register fewer than 3 months of published photographs on a single application.

In general, to obtain special remedies (that is, statutory damages and attorney fees), you need to register the work before any infringement takes place or within three months after the work's first publication. If you choose to invoke FL-124 for photography, however, your three-month grace period starts ticking from the date of publication for the earliest published photograph in the group.

Example. Your group contains twelve photographs, each published in a separate month of calendar year 2050 (one was published in January, one in February, etc.). You figure you'll wait until January 2051 to submit your group registration, in order to get the most for your $30 fee. If someone infringes any of these photographs after March 2050, though, you're precluded from claiming statutory damages or attorney fees because your three-month grace period started ticking in January 2050.

Leaf Me Alone:
First Sale and Derivative Works

national Public Radio (NPR) carried a story about an innovative photographer who works in chlorophyll. He prints his negatives on leaves gathered from his mother's garden.

....

COPYRIGHT (FIRST
SALE DOCTRINE)

COPYRIGHT
(DERIVATIVE
WORKS)

COPYRIGHT
(ORIGINALITY
REQUIREMENT)

MUNOZ V.
ALBUQUERQUE
A.R.T CO.

ANNIE LEE V. DECK
THE WALLS, INC.

Well, he prints negatives on leaves. Whether they're his or not remains to be seen. The NPR report suggests that he uses images from magazines and online archives. We'll give this artist the benefit of the doubt and assume he has appropriate licenses from the copyright owners of these images. For purposes of discussion, though – what if he doesn't? Is it OK to lift an image from a magazine, or from the internet, and print it on a leaf?

My view is no, it's not OK. I see no difference between printing the image onto a leaf and printing the image onto a piece of paper. It's still copying; it's still reproducing the image, which is something only a copyright owner may do (see Figure 1).

What happens, though, if the artist (or anyone else) were to purchase an image, affix it to a leaf and then offer it for sale? Please note: I said, "affix," not "copy."

In this conversation we explore copyright law's **first sale doctrine** and the concept of **derivative works**.

The first sale doctrine is a provision of copyright law stating that once a buyer has purchased a particular copy of a work, the buyer can dispose of that copy by sale or any other means (17 USC §109). The buyer does not acquire any copyright interest in the work (see Conversation #9). With certain limitations, however, the buyer may dispose of the particular item(s) she purchased in any way she happens to see fit. This applies whether the "copy" in her possession is a one-of-a-kind original or one in a series of multiples. If there's only one copy, the doctrine applies. If there are thousands of copies, the doctrine applies to each individual copy.

Last century (in the 1980s and 1990s) a company known as ART purchased multiple copies of an artistic image, affixed each copy to a ceramic tile and offered the individual tiles for sale. ART did this quite a lot and, consequently, got sued for copyright infringement by several artists. The artists claimed that ART's tiles were **derivative works** of their images and, since only a copyright owner can make a derivative work (see Figure 1), creating the tiles constituted infringement.

ART replied, "Hey. We lawfully purchased each and every copy we put on a tile. The first sale doctrine says we can dispose of our copies however we wish. We chose to put them on tiles and dispose of them by sale. That's not infringement."

Query: Who's right? (OK, that's a loaded question.)

Better phrased: Who prevailed?

Answer: The artists…and then ART Co.

Section 101 of the Copyright Act defines "derivative work" as follows:

> A "derivative work" is a work based upon one or more preexisting works,

such as a translation, musical arrangement, dramatization, fictionalization, motion picture version, sound recording, art reproduction, abridgment, condensation, or any other form in which a work may be recast, transformed, or adapted. A work consisting of editorial revisions, annotations, elaborations, or other modifications, which, as a whole, represent an original work of authorship, is a "derivative work."

In 1993 a Federal court found that ART's tiles were, in fact, derivative works (*Munoz v. Albuquerque A.R.T. Co.* 829 F Supp 309 [D. Alaska 1993], *affd* 38 F 3d 1218 [9th Cir. 1994). ART had argued that placing the images on tiles was merely a form of display, akin to framing, and that this practice neither "reproduced," "recast," "transformed" nor "adapted" the images. The court disagreed, noting:

It is commonly understood that [framing] amounts to only a method of display.... [I]t is a relatively simple matter to remove the print or painting and display it differently if the owner chooses to do so. [But] neither of these things is true of the art work affixed to a ceramic tile.... [T]iles lend themselves to other uses such as trivets (individually) or wall coverings (collectively).

The court essentially found that using epoxy resin to bind a legitimately-acquired image to ceramic tile constituted creation of a derivative work and, thus, infringement. In the court's view, once someone modifies a piece of artwork for any use other than that which the artist originally intended (e.g., for use as a trivet rather than as a notecard), the work has been sufficiently "transformed" or "recast" so as to constitute a derivative work.

Let's review §101 and the definition of "derivative work" (above). If the definition ended after that first sentence, it would be much easier to defend the *Munoz* deci-

Originality is a statutory and constitutional prerequisite for copyright protection.

• •

sion. The second sentence, however, states that a derivative (secondary) work consists of modifications *which, as a whole, represent an original work of authorship*. As later courts subsequently held, the changes or modifications must, themselves, qualify for copyright protection as "original works of authorship." If they do not, the secondary work is not a derivative of the original and, consequently, it does not infringe upon the original.

In 1996 ART defended another Federal court action in which the issues were substantially the same as they'd been in *Munoz*. This time, however, the presiding judge found for ART, holding that the tiles were not infringements (*Annie Lee, et al. v. Deck the Walls, Inc. and A.R.T. Company*, 925 F Supp 576 [N.D. Illinois 1996], *affd* 125 F 3d 580 [7th Cir. 1997]). In reaching this conclusion, the court found no legal distinction between displaying art in a frame or on a tile. In the court's view:

...the only relevant inquiry...is whether ART's ceramic tile process transforms, adapts or recasts [the artist's] original work into a new and different original work...[and] whether the new 'work,' the ceramic tile, contains sufficient originality, as required by the Constitution and the Copyright Act.

Originality is a statutory and constitutional prerequisite for copyright protection. The United States Supreme Court has held consistently that while the threshold for originality is low, originality is the *sine qua non* of copyright. (Translation: ya gotta have it.) How low can you go before failing to meet the "threshold"? According to the Supreme Court: "Originality requires only that the author display some minimum level of creativity (*Feist Publications, Inc.* v. *Rural Telephone Service Co., Inc.*, 499 U.S. 340; 111 S. Ct. 1282; 113 L. Ed. 2d 358 [1991]).

Back to *Annie Lee*. The court found:

The mundane act of placing notecards onto a ceramic tile falls into the narrow category of works in which no creative spark exists. Thus, the ceramic tiles are not a new and different original work, but the same exact work placed onto a different background. ART did not display any creativity in gluing [the artist's] work onto the separate surface….No intellectual effort or creativity was necessary to transfer the notecard to the tile.

The court noted, as well, that following the *Munoz* determination (that ART's tiles were derivative works) ART attempted to register the tile design with the Copyright Office – and its application was rejected as not copyrightable because the tiles contained no original artistic expression. The *Annie Lee* court further observed that the artist could have prevented ART from making and selling the tiles by refusing in the first instance to sell so many copies to ART. Finally, in response to the artist's argument that ART engaged in unfair competition by selling her work on their tiles, the court simply observed that nothing prevented the artist herself from doing the exact same thing.

Annie Lee was upheld on appeal by the Seventh Circuit Court of Appeals. In its decision the Seventh Circuit contributed these observations:

> If the framing process does not create a derivative work, then mounting art on a tile, which serves as a flush frame, does not create a derivative work.

> If mounting work on a tile amounts to "transfiguration" then so would changing a painting's frame or a photograph's mat – and clearly those actions do not constitute legal transfiguration.

> The artist's work, on ART's tiles, was not "recast, adapted or transformed" because the tiles still depicted exactly what the art depicted when it left the artist's studio.

At the time *Annie Lee* was decided, the Federal circuit courts (see Conversation #19) remained at odds over whether ART's "tiling" process constituted infringement. Some sided with the Seventh Circuit and some stuck with the reasoning of *Munoz*. Over time the Seventh Circuit's view came to prevail, however, and now most Federal courts would adopt this approach when faced with similar facts. In the majority of circuits, therefore, artists should understand that when someone purchases a copy of your work, displays that copy in a manner you had not foreseen and then sells it to someone else: it's not necessarily infringement.

artists should understand that when someone purchases a copy of your work, displays that copy in a manner you had not foreseen and then sells it to someone else: it's not necessarily infringement.

The State and Federal Courts

 n interesting copyright decision from the Seventh Circuit Court of Appeals involves June Toney, a model whose likeness appeared in advertisements for L'Oreal® and Wella® hair care products (*Toney* v. *L'Oreal U.S.A., Inc.,* et al., 384 F.3d 486 [7th Cir. 2004]).

TONEY V. L'OREAL U.S.A., INC.

ALTERNATIVE DISPUTE RESOLUTION

JURISDICTION

VENUE

STATE AND FEDERAL COURT SYSTEMS

The topic of this conversation might surprise you. It's not about copyright; it's not about advertising. It's not even about hair care products. In this conversation we chat not about the court's decision, but about the court itself.

Do you know what Federal circuit you live in?

Please welcome "Q," an inquisitive artist, and "A," a pedantic attorney with a troubling sense of humor. In recent weeks Q and a gallery owner have been arguing about payments due to Q under a **consignment** agreement. The owner had not wanted to use a written contract but Q, a savvy Reader, insisted. Unfortunately, instead of retaining legal counsel to draft the agreement, Q and the gallery used a "canned" contract downloaded from the internet (see Conversation #13).

They got what they paid for. The canned contract had no provision for **alternative dispute resolution**; nor did it specify a **jurisdiction** or **venue** in the event of **litigation**.

Fade in to an increasingly frenzied Q and the predictably smug A:

Q: I can't let the gallery get away with this. What should I do?

A: You lookin' at me?

Q: Get over it, would you? I learned my lesson with the internet contract. Now come on…what do we do?

A: Well, there's mediation and arbitration, two methods of alternative dispute resolution, or "ADR." Your contract doesn't provide for ADR, though, so unless the gallery agrees voluntarily, or we find a state or Federal arbitration law directly applicable to this dispute, you probably can't force them into mediation or arbitration.

Q: They'll never agree.

A: Then you'll have to sue. How much money do they owe you?

Q: $624,000

A: So much for small claims court. Where's the gallery?

Q: New York City.

A: And you live in New York too, right?

Q: No, I live across the river in New Jersey. Why?

A: We have to decide where to bring the lawsuit.

Q: You mean, in New York or New Jersey?

A: I mean in state court or Federal court.

Q: See ya.

Q leaves the room.

Q knew (from experience) that A was about to launch into a tedious lecture on distinctions between the state and Federal court systems. Q didn't have time for the speech.

"Let A earn her money," thought Q, "I have art to make."

Q's choice (to exit the conversation) is understandable. State and Federal court jurisdiction is extraordinarily complex and absolutely the attorney's domain. On the other hand, all professional artists should have a basic understanding of the courts as part of their art law knowledge base.

As you may recall from Miss Finney's civics class, the United States Constitution establishes three separate branches of Federal government: the legislative, the executive and the judicial. The legislative (Congress) makes the laws; the executive branch enforces the laws; and the Federal courts (the judicial branch) interpret and apply the laws.

In addition to our Federal courts, each US state has its own separate court system. Although the names and functions vary, state court systems typically have at least a trial-level court, an "intermediate-level" appeals court and a "top-level" appeals court.

Federal courts are set up pretty similarly. The United States is divided into 13 geographic "circuits," each with a trial-level court called the "District Court," an intermediate-level appeals court called the "Circuit Court" and a top-level appeals court: the United States Supreme Court.

> **In general, state courts hear matters arising under state law and Federal courts hear matters arising under Federal law.**

Both state and Federal courts also have trial courts for "specialty" issues, such as small claims, bankruptcy, etc.

In general (and this is a sweeping generalization to which there are many exceptions), state courts hear matters arising under state law and Federal courts hear matters arising under Federal law. Consignment agreements are contracts, and contracts are typically matters of state law. It was reasonable, therefore, for Q to have assumed A would bring the lawsuit in state court and that the only question was whether the appropriate state would be New York or New Jersey.

Let us pause. **Why did Q assume that New York and New Jersey were the only available state courts?** Could A bring the lawsuit in Colorado? Alabama? Tibet? Probably not, and here by way of explanation is a full semester of law school in two easy paragraphs. (Note how the word "jurisdiction" has three different meanings!)

In order to hear your matter, the court you choose must have **jurisdiction** (in this context, meaning control) over the person you are suing. This is called "personal jurisdiction." In order to establish personal jurisdiction you (the **plaintiff**) need to show the court that the person you are suing (the **defendant**) has some sort of minimum contacts with the **jurisdiction** (in this context, meaning the state) in which the court sits. You can generally establish minimum contacts by showing that the defendant resides in the jurisdiction, owns property there, does business there, signed your contract there, etc.

The court you choose must also have **jurisdiction** (in this context, meaning authority) over the type of matter you are bringing. This is called "subject matter jurisdiction." Think back to A's comment about small claims court. Small claims courts are typically limited in "subject matter jurisdiction" to matters involving… small claims, i.e., matters where the amount in controversy is less than $5000 or some other relatively small amount (the actual threshold varies from state to state). In Q's matter, the amount in controversy is quite large. Accordingly, A will have to bring the lawsuit in a court with "subject matter jurisdiction" over matters involving larger amounts of money.

OK. So Colorado, Alabama and Tibet are probably out unless Q can establish that the gallery has some sort of minimum contacts with those jurisdictions. If A brings Q's lawsuit in state court, A will likely choose either New York (where the gallery is located) or New Jersey (if the gallery has any contacts with New Jersey, which it probably does.) The lawsuit could definitely move forward in an appropriate state court. **Why, then, was A talking about bringing it in Federal court?**

To bring the lawsuit in a Federal district court (rather than a state trial-level court) A would need to establish that the Federal court has "subject matter jurisdiction" over the matter. There are several types of Federal subject matter jurisdiction. The two most common are known as "Federal question" jurisdiction, which exists when the controversy arises under Federal law or the United States Constitution; and "diversity of citizenship" jurisdiction. The "diversity" statute provides:

> *The district courts shall have original jurisdiction of all civil actions where the matter in controversy exceeds the sum or value of $75,000, exclusive of interest and costs, and is between –*
>
> *citizens of different States....*

28 USC §1332.

We've already established that Q's dispute arises under state law — so "Federal question" jurisdiction is probably not available.

Because the gallery is in New York and Q resides in New Jersey, however, and because the amount in controversy exceeds $75,000, A recognized that diversity jurisdiction might apply, making Federal court a potential alternative for Q's lawsuit.

Quiz: There are Federal district courts in New York and in New Jersey and, for that matter, all over the United States. Assuming A opts for Federal court, could A bring the lawsuit in any district court, anywhere?

No. And herein lies the difference between **jurisdiction** and **venue.** We've already established that the Federal district court has subject matter jurisdiction over Q's matter. That jurisdiction is "system-wide.", i.e. a Federal district court sitting in Alabama would have subject matter jurisdiction over Q's matter. It would not, however, be an appropriate venue. In addition to jurisdiction rules, there are also venue rules restricting – from among the class of all courts at a certain level (e.g., all Federal district courts) – the field of particular courts (e.g., the Federal district courts sitting in New Jersey or New York) in which a litigant may bring an action. Usually, venue is determined by factors such as residence of the parties or where the disputed transaction took place (see, for example, 28 USC §1391).

Plain English summary:

Figure out which type of court (e.g., state court, Federal district court, small claims court, bankruptcy court, etc.) has both personal jurisdiction over the defendant and subject matter jurisdiction over the controversy.

Then, once you've identified the proper type of court, figure out which specific court of that type (e.g., state court sitting in X county, state court sitting in Y county, Federal district court sitting in Z state, etc.) has "venue".

Had Q not left the room so abruptly, Q would now understand that Federal "district court" refers to a Federal trial-level court and that a decision from the "Seventh Circuit" refers to the Federal intermediate-level appeals court located...where? (*Hint:* http://www.uscourts.gov/images/CircuitMap.pdf)

Now do you know what Federal circuit you live in?

To learn about the names, functions and subject matter jurisdiction of your own state courts, these websites are informative:

http://www.uslegalforms.com/lawdigest/state-courts.htm

http://www.ncsconline.org/D_KIS/info_court_web_sites.html

The Visual Artists Rights Act:
A "Banner" Decision Restricts Moral Rights

VARA" is an acronym for the Visual Artists Rights Act of 1990 (17 USC §106A), an amendment to the United States Copyright Act designed to protect artists' **moral rights**. Moral rights involve the artist's personal (as opposed to economic) interest in receiving attribution for his or her work and in preserving the integrity of the work, even after it has been sold or licensed.

POLLARA V.
SEYMOUR

VISUAL ARTISTS
RIGHTS ACT

MORAL RIGHTS

VARA provides that the author of a "work of visual art" shall have the right, for life,

> *to prevent any intentional distortion, mutilation or other modification of that work which would be prejudicial to his or her honor or reputation…[and]*

> *to prevent any destruction of a work of recognized stature, and any intentional or grossly negligent destruction of that work is a violation of that right.*

17 USC §§ 106A(a)(3), (d)(3)

VARA suffers from significant limitations in its scope and application. The biggest limitation is the Copyright Act's definition of "work of visual art:"

> *A painting, drawing, print or sculpture, existing in a single copy, in a limited edition of 200 copies or fewer that are signed and consecutively numbered by the author, or, in the case of a sculpture, in multiple cast, carved, or fabricated sculptures of 200 or fewer that are consecutively numbered by the author and bear the signature or other identifying mark of the author; or*

> *a still photographic image produced for exhibition purposes only, existing in a single copy that is signed by the author, or in a limited edition of 200 copies or fewer that are signed and consecutively numbered by the author.*

> *A work of visual art does not include —*

> *(A)*

> *(i) any poster, map, globe, chart, technical drawing, diagram, model, applied art, motion picture or other audiovisual work, book, magazine, newspaper, periodical, data base, electronic information service, electronic publication, or similar publication;*

> *(ii) any merchandising item or advertising, promotional, descriptive, covering, or packaging material or container;*

> *(iii) any portion or part of any item described in clause (i) or (ii);*

> *any work made for hire; or*

> *any work not subject to copyright protection under this title.*

17 USC §101

Here are some other limitations:

Regarding distortion, mutilation and modification: (a) the work has to fall within the definition of "work of visual art;" and (b) the distortion, mutilation or modification has to be intentional; and (c) the distortion, mutilation or modification has to be prejudicial to the artist's honor or reputation.

Regarding destruction: (a) the work has to fall within the definition of "work of visual art;" and (b) the work has to be of recognized stature; and (c) the destruction has to be intentional or grossly negligent.

VARA litigation is relatively rare, and court decisions few, because of these limitations. In the vast majority of cases VARA is simply unavailable or inapplicable to an artist's facts and circumstances. Consequently, when the Federal courts do issue VARA decisions, they merit our attention. Every case, after all, plays an important role in shaping the development of moral rights in the United States.

In 2003 the United States Court of Appeals for the Second Circuit issued a VARA decision in the matter of *Pollara* v. *Seymour, 344 F 3d 265* (2d Cir. 2003). Legal scholars agree (OK, my law clerks and I agree) the decision further restricts the scope of VARA and artists' moral rights.

Joanne Pollara is an artist from Albany, New York. The Gideon Coalition, a non-profit group that promotes and offers low-cost legal services, commissioned Pollara to create a large banner for Gideon's display table at a special event known as "Lobbying Day."[9] Pollara spent more than 100 hours creating the banner, which ended up being ten feet high by thirty feet long. Pollara applied latex paint to heavy-gauge photographer's paper and reinforced the edges with duct tape. According to the Second Circuit,

> The completed banner, in three or four colors, depicts a tableau of two dozen stylized people, with few salient features, standing on line against a background of shut doors labeled "PUBLIC DEFENDER," "LEGAL AID," and "PRISONERS LEGAL SERVICES." They patiently await entry, at left, of an open door marked "LAWYER," inside which sits a person, wearing a jacket and tie…. Many of the people on line are depicted to suggest different ethnicities…. Large lettering across the top and left read: "EXECUTIVE BUDGET THREATENS RIGHT TO COUNSEL" and "PRESERVE THE RIGHT TO COUNSEL – NOW MORE THAN EVER!"

Lobbying Day was scheduled to take place in Albany's Empire State Plaza, a complex of distinctive buildings housing the New York State Legislature and other government offices. On Lobbying Day Eve, Pollara and several helpers erected the banner in an enclosed, indoor public space at the Plaza. When it was in place they went home, leaving the banner unattended.

Here's the thing about Albany and, in fairness, most capitol cities. They're sticklers for the rules, and they have a lot of them. In order to place a banner in the Empire State Plaza one needs a certain type of permit; to leave it overnight you need yet another. Gideon had failed to obtain either. Squat. No permits. (Not the greatest endorsement for an organization offering to help others with their legal needs…but I digress.)

Later that evening a Plaza security person noticed the banner and alerted his supervisor. The supervisor made a personal inspection, determined that no permits were in place and instructed his staff to remove the banner. They did so and, in the process, tore the banner vertically into three pieces. The next morning Pollara found her banner lying torn and crumpled in a corner of the supervisor's office. Long story short, she sued under VARA.

Defendants (the State of New York and the supervisor) argued that Pollara's banner wasn't entitled to VARA protection because, in their view, it was really a "poster," and posters are not "works of visual art" under the statute. The District court disagreed, citing the dictionary definition of "poster:" a large printed placard used for the purpose of advertising or publicity. Pollara's banner was a single, hand-painted work and therefore not a "poster."

In its next breath, though, the District court dismissed Pollara's case. The court found the banner was not a "work of visual art" after all: not because it was a "poster" but, rather, because it contained "advertising or promotional material," and its purpose was to attract public attention to Gideon's table.

> **The court found the banner was not a "work of visual art" after all: not because it was a "poster" but, rather, because it contained "advertising or promotional material."**

The District court further determined that even if the banner had been a "work of visual art," it wasn't of "recognized stature" and thus not entitled to VARA's protections. Pollara appealed to the Second Circuit Court of Appeals.

The Second Circuit found, first off, that the District court blew it on the "recognized stature" issue. According to VARA a work only needs to be of "recognized stature" if the issue is the work's destruction. The VARA section affording protection against mutilation or modification contains no such limitation. Pollara had sued under both sections: the one addressing destruction and the one addressing mutilation and modification – so the fact that her banner was not of "recognized stature" was no reason for throwing her out of court.

The Second Circuit agreed, however, that the banner contained advertising material, thus rendering it ineligible for classification as a "work of visual art." Pollara argued that the "speech" on the banner, though admittedly for promotional purposes, was non-commercial; in her view Congress only intended to exclude commercial advertising from VARA's scope. Pollara provided no evidence of such Congressional intent, however, and as the Court observed, VARA on its face makes no distinction between commercial and non-commercial speech.

The Second Circuit could have "left it at that" and simply dismissed the appeal. Instead, the court offered a lengthy explanation leaving no room for doubt or argument that VARA protects nothing that's used for advertising or promotion, regardless of the commercial or non-commercial nature of the cause or business the work of art promotes.

What, then, of a work (such as a painting commissioned to promote the Olympics or a sculpture to promote AIDS awareness) created originally for purposes of promotion that later in its life becomes a mainstream work of art? Can such a work ever acquire status as a "work of visual art" under VARA? One judge on the *Pollara* panel thinks so; the rest of the court disagrees. In the majority's view: once promotional, always promotional. To hold otherwise would require courts to become judges not of the law, but of a work's artistic merit. And that, holds the court, would be a "dangerous undertaking."

The *Pollara* decision applies directly only to VARA cases decided within the Second Circuit's jurisdiction (New York, Connecticut and Vermont). Because there are so few VARA cases, though, and because the Second Circuit is a leader in art law jurisprudence, other Federal courts will consider *Pollara* in similar matters. In consequence, the trend restricting VARA's scope – rather than expanding it – is likely to continue.

---

[9] I used to live in Albany, New York, and I can tell you from experience that in Albany, every day is lobbying day. That aside, the astute Reader might think, "Hmm. A nonprofit organization… lobbying… isn't that a problem?" It depends. Tax exempt organizations aren't totally prohibited from lobbying, but they must observe extremely strict regulations limiting the amount of time they spend trying to "influence legislation;" otherwise they risk losing their tax-exempt status.

Copyright Duration: You Do the Math

for years, copyright lasted for the life of the author plus fifty years. Pursuant to the Copyright Term Extension Act of 1998 (CTEA), Congress extended the duration from life of the author plus fifty years, to life plus seventy.[10]

ELDRED V. ASHCROFT

COPYRIGHT TERM EXTENSION ACT OF 1998

PUBLIC DOMAIN

CALCULATING COPYRIGHT DURATION

In January 2003 the United States Supreme Court issued its decision in *Eldred* v. *Ashcroft* (537 U.S. 186; 123 S. Ct. 769; 154 L. Ed. 2d 683 [2003]), a case challenging the constitutionality of the CTEA. With Justices Breyer and Stevens dissenting, a majority of the Court upheld the CTEA, finding that Congress acted within its constitutional authority by extending the duration of copyright protection, both for existing and future works.

Much has been written about the *Eldred* decision. In this conversation I will summarize the decision's principal points, but I will do so briefly. This isn't going to be an exposition on constitutional law. Instead, we're going to examine the day-to-day nuts and bolts of copyright duration. In short, we're going to do math.

But first, a few words about *Eldred*. The CTEA tacked on an additional 20 years to the term of copyright, both for existing work already subject to copyright protection, and for work yet to be created ("future work"). In *Eldred*, challengers conceded that extending the term for future work was within Congress' authority, because the U.S. Constitution permits Congress to enact legislation "securing [to Authors] *for limited Times* ...the exclusive Right to their...Writings" (US Const, art I, §8, cl 8; emphasis supplied; capitalization in original; see http://www.house.gov/Constitution/Constitution.html). There can be no argument that the span of time defined as "life of the author plus seventy years" is a finite, limited term.

The challengers contended, however, that applying the extension to existing work, for which the duration "clock" had already started ticking, violated the Constitution's "limited Times" provision. The "limited Time" in effect when a copyright is secured, they argued, "becomes the constitutional boundary, a clear line beyond the power of Congress to extend" (*Eldred* v. *Ashcroft*, 537 U.S. 186, 193). The Supreme Court disagreed, finding that if life plus seventy is a "limited Time" for future work, it's also a "limited Time" for existing work.

As the Court noted, Congress has extended the term of copyright numerous times since enactment of the Constitution's copyright clause in 1790 (most notably in 1831 and 1909), and in all cases the extensions applied to existing, as well as future works. It's easy to assail the Court's reasoning, i.e., "since nobody challenged it before it must be OK...." As promised, however, that's not the focus of this conversation. The law of the land is now quite firmly "life of the author plus seventy years," and artists need to know how to calculate copyright duration.

Let's fire up the calculators.

January 1, 1978 to present. "Life plus seventy" applies to works created and fixed in a tangible medium of expression on or after January 1, 1978. If the work happens to be a **joint work** in which two or more authors share the copyright (see Conversation #10), the term lasts for 70 years after the death of the last surviving author. Copyright protection for **work made for hire** (see Conversations #10 and

#11), as well as anonymous and pseudonymous works, is 95 years from first publication or 120 years from creation, whichever is shorter.

Congress amended the Copyright Act in 1976. The 1976 amendments (which became effective on January 1, 1978) did away with the previous requirement that, in order to secure copyright protection, a work had either to be published or registered with the Copyright Office. Now all an author has to do to get copyright protection is to fix her work in a "tangible medium of expression," e.g., write it down, put it on canvas, record it, etc.

Pre-January 1, 1978. Prior to the 1976 amendments copyright only lasted for 28 years. In order to obtain a second 28-year term (extending the total term of protection to 56 years), an author had to renew his copyright with the Copyright Office – and he could do so only in the 28th year of the first term. If the author failed to renew within that narrow window of time, the work passed into the public domain.

The 1976 amendments tacked on an additional 39 years to the renewal term, bringing the total term of copyright protection from 56 years (28 plus 28, as above) to 95 years (28 years in the first term plus 67 years [28 plus 39] in the renewal term.) Until a subsequent amendment in 1992 you still had to renew your copyright in order to get those 67 extra years. After the 1992 amendments, renewal became automatic.

All of this ancient history actually matters, today. Suppose, for example, you wish to incorporate a photograph in your work. If the photograph is a post-1977 work, you know that its copyright lasts for the life of the photographer plus seventy years, and it will not fall into the public domain until then. If the photograph was taken before January 1, 1978, though, you need to know about all of these prior rules and amendments, and which one(s) apply to the work in question.

> When copyright duration is at issue, your first question should be whether the work was published before 1923. If so, it's in the public domain. Chances are you'll be dealing with more recent works, however, in which case the cardinal question is whether the work was created before or after January 1, 1978.

Our conversation so far has addressed pre-1978 work that that was properly published or registered with the Copyright Office. What about pre-1978 work that had not been properly published or registered?

Work that had been created, but neither published nor registered before January 1, 1978, automatically "got" copyright protection under the 1976 amendments. And in general, such work is also subject to the "life plus seventy" rule. As a perk, however, all such pre-1978 "non-published, non-registered" work got a guaranteed period of protection for 25 years and a "free pass" until December 31, 2002. So the copyright for work in this category lasted for "life plus seventy" or until December 31, 2002, whichever was greater. And to make matters even more complicated, if the work happened to get published between January 1, 1978 and December 31, 2002 it got another 45 years, extending the copyright to "life plus seventy" or December 31, 2047, whichever is greater.

By now you're probably getting the picture: calculating copyright duration is not a simple task. I didn't even describe the old notice requirement (see Conversation #16) or the special rules for work originally copyrighted between January 1, 1950 and December 31, 1963!

When copyright duration is at issue, your first question should be whether the work was published before 1923. If so, it's in the public domain. Chances are you'll be dealing with more recent works, however, in which case the cardinal question is whether the work was created before or after January 1, 1978. If the work was created on or after that date, and there is a single author, you're dealing with the familiar "life plus seventy." If the work was created before January 1, 1978, if it's a work made for hire or if there is more than one author involved, be aware that calculating the applicable term requires in-depth familiarity with a long history of Congressional amendments.

To learn more about copyright duration, consult the Copyright Office's Circular 15a (http://www.copyright.gov/circs/circ15a.pdf). For more on the Court's analysis of the *Eldred* case, see: http://eon.law.harvard.edu/openlaw/eldredvashcroft/. The decision itself is available online at: http://www.supremecourtus.gov/opinions/opinions.html.

And as always, if there's more at stake than you can afford to lose, consult competent legal counsel.

---

[10] Congress did so at the behest of the late former Rep. Sonny Bono who, many believe, championed the extension at the behest of corporate giants (eek, it's a mouse!) whose valuable copyrights were about to expire.

United We Stand:
Go Directly to Jail

Patriotism. It's often reflected in our art, so let's discuss the many ways that using national symbols can land us in the slammer.

The provisions that follow appear in Chapter 33 of Title 18 of the **United States Code**. Title 18 is entitled, "Crimes and Criminal Procedure." Chapter 33 is entitled, "Emblems, Insignia and Names." Anyone who violates these provisions is subject to a fine, imprisonment of not more than six months, or both. In this conversation I offer plain English summaries mixed, perhaps, with a bit of editorial comment. Exact statutory language is available online at http://www4.law.cornell .edu/ uscode/

§701: Official badges, identification cards, other insignia

The heads of United States departments and agencies prescribe the design for badges, identification cards and other insignia used by their officers and employees. If, without authority, you manufacture, sell or possess any badge or ID card bearing that design, or if you make any engraving, photograph, print or impression in the likeness of any such badge or ID card, you go directly to jail. (OK, you might just get a fine, but imprisonment is a possibility, so grant me the dramatic license.)

§702: Uniform of armed forces and Public Health Service

You can't wear the uniform or anything similar to a "distinctive part of the uniform" of the armed forces of the United States anywhere within the jurisdiction of the United States or the Canal Zone, without authority to do so. If you do: see ya in six months. And note, intent to violate the provision is not a prerequisite for conviction.

In 1944 a 74-year-old man proudly wore the uniform of a captain in the United States Army to a social dinner. He honestly believed he was entitled to wear the uniform, but in fact he was not. A United States Federal court found him guilty, notwithstanding his belief in the propriety of his conduct (*Gaston* v. *United States*, 143 F.2d 10 [D.C. Cir. 1944]). The courts have upheld exceptions to this provision for actors wearing military uniforms in theatrical productions, so it bears observing that if a protected First Amendment interest is involved, there can be exceptions to this restriction. Artists would be well advised to seek counsel on this issue before taking the risk, however, particularly in today's highly charged political climate.

§703: Uniform of friendly nation

Unlike §702, inadvertent behavior won't get you in trouble. However, if you wear the uniform or regalia of a foreign nation with which the United States is at peace and you do so "with intent to deceive or mislead," you violate the law. Curiously, the statute says nothing about wearing the uniform of an unfriendly nation. (If you're dumb enough to do that, though, you'd likely be arrested on other grounds altogether!)

§704: Military medals or decorations

You may not wear, manufacture or sell any decoration or medal authorized by Congress for the armed forces of the United States. Six months in the slammer. And if that decoration or medal happens to be the Congressional Medal of Honor: you go away for a full year.

§705: Badge or medal of veterans' organizations

This provision involves badges, medals, emblems and other insignia of veterans' organizations and their auxiliaries. If you knowingly manufacture, reproduce, sell or purchase such items for resale, you break the law. Imprisonment looms if, without authority, you knowingly print, lithograph, engrave or otherwise reproduce the designs on any poster, circular, periodical, magazine, newspaper or other publication; you also risk prosecution if you circulate or distribute any printed matter bearing a reproduction of such badge, medal, emblem or other insignia.

§706: Red Cross

You may not wear or display the sign of the Red Cross for the fraudulent purpose of inducing the belief that you are a member or agent for the American National Red Cross; nor may you use the emblem of the Greek red cross on a white ground, or the words "Red Cross" or "Geneva Cross" or any combination of those words.

§707: 4-H club emblem fraudulently used

It's a fine and/or prison if, with intent to defraud, you wear or display the sign or emblem of the 4-H clubs, consisting of a green four-leaf clover with stem, and the letter H in white or gold on each leaflet.

It's a fine and/or prison if, with intent to defraud, you wear or display the sign or emblem of the 4-H clubs, consisting of a green four-leaf clover with stem, and the letter H in white or gold on each leaflet. It's also a crime to use any such sign or emblem or the words "4-H Club" or "4-H Clubs" or any combination of those words or characters. The only people authorized to use these words and emblems are 4-H clubs, representatives of the United States Department of Agriculture (http://www.usda.gov/wps/portal/usdahome), land grant colleges and persons authorized by the Secretary of Agriculture.

§708: Swiss Confederation coat of arms

No person or entity may use the coat of arms of the Swiss Confederation, consisting of an upright white cross with equal arms and lines on a red ground, as a trademark or commercial label or as an advertisement or insignia for any business or organization or for any trade or commercial purpose.

§711: "Smokey Bear" character or name

Do not even think about using the name or character "Smokey Bear" before consulting the rules and regulations of the Secretary of Agriculture and consulting with the Association of State Foresters (http://www.stateforesters.org) and the Advertising Council (http://www.adcouncil.org).

§711a: "Woodsy Owl" character, name or slogan

Same goes for "Woodsy Owl" and Woodsy's famous slogan, "Give a Hoot, Don't Pollute."

§713: Use of likenesses of the great seal of the United States, the seals of the President and Vice President, the seal of the United States Senate, the seal of the United States House of Representatives, and the seal of the United States Congress

You can't display or print any of these seals in or in connection with any advertisement, poster, circular, book, pamphlet or other publication, public meeting, play, motion picture, telecast or other production, or on any building, monument or stationery for the purpose of conveying a false impression of sponsorship or approval by the Government of the United States. Nor may you manufacture, reproduce, sell or purchase for resale any likeness of such seals.

§715: "The Golden Eagle Insignia"

The Golden Eagle Insignia is defined in the United States Code as the representation of an American Golden Eagle (colored gold) and a family group (colored midnight blue) enclosed within a circle (colored white with a midnight blue border) framed by a rounded triangle (colored gold with a midnight blue border). Except as authorized under the rules and regulations of the Secretary of the Interior (http://www.doi.gov/welcome.html), anyone who knowingly manufacturers, reproduces or uses the Golden Eagle Insignia is subject to prosecution, fine and/or imprisonment.

§716: Police badges

You may not transfer, transport or receive a counterfeit police badge, nor may you transfer a genuine police badge to an individual, knowing that such individual is not authorized to possess it. It is a defense to prosecution under this section, though, if the badge is used or is intended to be used exclusively as a memento, in a collection or exhibit, for decorative purposes, for a dramatic presentation such as a theatrical, film or television production, or for any other recreational purpose.

That leaves the most controversial symbol of all, the flag. Section 700 of Chapter 33 is entitled, "Desecration of the flag of the United States; penalties." As most Readers are aware, flag desecration statutes have been held unconstitutional by the United States Supreme Court (see *Texas* v. *Johnson*, 491 US 397 [1989]; *United States* v. *Eichman*, 496 US 310 [1990]). The flag has played a prominent role in contemporary art and its use as a medium of expression has sparked heated constitutional debate. Entering "flag desecration" into any major search engine will yield a plethora of resources to inform this ongoing discussion.

> Except as authorized under the rules and regulations of the Secretary of the Interior, anyone who knowingly manufacturers, reproduces or uses the Golden Eagle Insignia is subject to prosecution, fine and/or imprisonment.

Trademark Basics

adison, Wisconsin's "Art Fair on the Square" is awesome.[11] Hundreds of thousands of people stroll beneath brilliant blue skies listening to music, noshing on bratwurst, spending money on art.

I look for legal problems.

Booth #17.[12] An artist identifies his business with two catchy slogans, both of which appear on his signs followed by the familiar "™" symbol (thought by many to mean, "trademark"). Of these two usages, one is appropriate and one is not. I mention this to the artist and he replies, "well, they're not real trademarks anyway."

Very true. So why bother?

A trademark identifies the source of goods and services. When José Consumer sees/hears/smells your trademark, your product comes to mind. José doesn't think about your competitor's product. He thinks about yours. Why? Because an effective trademark sets your product apart from others. Consider the following exchange:

> Server: "My name is Raymond and I'll be your server. Can I get you something to drink?"
>
> Me: "I'd like a Diet X, please."
>
> Raymond: "Is Diet Y OK?"
>
> Me *(silently, to myself)*: "No!"
>
> Me *(out loud, to Raymond)*: "Yes."

I didn't ask for a cola. I asked for a particular cola: Diet X. And I know well enough that I'd rather have Diet X than Diet Y. Trademarks build brand loyalty and serve as representations of quality assurance. If I order something called Diet X I can be pretty sure that I'll get the product with which I am familiar.

Back to the artist in Booth 17. He was selling really cool mirrors shaped like footwear. [13] His first sign, referring to the mirrors, said, "Windows to the Sole™ ." That was OK. The second sign bore the artist's name and, referring to his artistry and business history, said, "Seeing Through To You, Since 1972™." Incorrect.

Quiz: Do you know why the first usage was appropriate and the second was not?

Recall what I said earlier in this conversation: *A trademark identifies the source of goods and services.* The United States Patent and Trademark Office (PTO) makes a distinction between products (goods) and services, and therefore so must we. If your mark refers to a product (like mirrors), it is appropriate to use the ™ symbol. If, however, your mark refers to a service (like presenting plays or creating art), then the mark is called a "servicemark" and the appropriate symbol is ˢᴹ instead of ™. So the artist's second sign should have read, "Seeing Through To You, Since 1972ˢᴹ."

Earlier I said the ™ symbol is "thought by many" to denote "trademark," my implication being: it really doesn't. Yet I just affirmed that ™ is OK, at least for products. What gives?

Well, having carefully explained the distinction between ™ and ᴿᴹ I'll now share another fun fact: neither symbol really means anything. (Isn't law great?)

If you want to protect your mark under United States trademark law (whether the mark be a trademark or a servicemark) you must apply to the PTO for a Federal registration. Unlike registering a copyright, which is inexpensive and comparatively easy, applying for Federal trademark/servicemark registration is expensive and a lot more complicated. You must apply in one or more of the "classes" that best describe your product or service, e.g., Class 28, Toys and sporting goods; Class 29, Meats and processed foods; Class 41, Education and entertainment, etc. You pay a nonrefundable filing fee of $335 for each class in which you apply. And there are a lot of legal principles that determine whether your mark is or is not entitled to a Federal registration. If you go ahead and apply, and it turns out your mark is not eligible for registration, you lose your filing fees.

If, however, you do obtain a Federal registration, you may then use the familiar ® symbol after your mark. (No one may ever use the ® symbol unless the PTO has issued a registration for the mark; see 22 USC §1111). The PTO makes a big deal during the application process about whether your mark is a trademark or a servicemark. Once you get your registration, though, you use the ® symbol either way. Go figure.

When people use ™ or ᴿᴹ after a mark, they do so to tell the world, "I don't have a Federal registration for this mark, but it's still mine and I intend to protect it." Perhaps you are pursuing Federal registration but the process (which takes close to a year under the best of circumstances) is not yet complete. Perhaps you know that your mark is not eligible for Federal protection, but you intend to protect it locally under state trademark or business competition laws. Neither ™ nor ᴿᴹ has any real legal significance. Used appropriately, however, the symbols are useful tools for placing others on notice that you have "claimed" the mark.

The mirror guy might sneer at this and huff, "so if neither ™ nor ᴿᴹ means anything, what's the big deal if I use the wrong one?" Point taken. It's not that big of a deal, if you're not really serious about protecting the mark. On the other hand, if you regard the mark as an important business asset and you are serious about protecting it, using the correct symbol boosts your credibility. It tells the world you've done your homework and you know what you're talking about. That alone might cause a potential infringer to think twice before appropriating your mark.

> ...if you regard the mark as an important business asset and you are serious about protecting it, using the correct symbol boosts your credibility. It tells the world you've done your homework and you know what you're talking about. That alone might cause a potential infringer to think twice before appropriating your mark.

It bears repeating: this is a complicated area and if you're thinking about applying for registration you should first obtain competent legal advice. In fact, you should seek such advice before you even select your mark. It's a bummer to invest a lot of time, money, marketing and goodwill in a trademark/servicemark only to find out later (when you're already in too deep) that that the mark will never be entitled to Federal protection.

For general information about the PTO and United States trademark procedure, check out the PTO website: http://www.uspto.gov/main/trademarks.htm

[11] http://www.madisonartcenter.org/events/special_artfair.html

[12] Booth numbers have been changed to protect the innocent.

[13] No he wasn't. This is entirely fictional. I invented the artist, his products and his slogans for purposes of illustration. Any resemblance to actual products or slogans is purely coincidental.

Using Trademarks in Your Art

i *f I depict a Samsonite suitcase in a painting, is that an infringement of the Samsonite Corporation's trademark?*

What happens when you use somebody else's trademark in your art?

This is a complicated issue. Think of it as an onion (and not just because it makes you cry.) Why? Because in order to analyze the issue, we need to peel away layers and layers of sub-issues before reaching the part we're really going to use.

Layer #1: Trademark Infringement. If you've depicted somebody else's trademark in your art, your first concern is likely to be trademark infringement. (*Am I infringing on the trademark? What does that mean? Am I going to get sued?*) Surprisingly, however, of the legal "layers" we need to consider, trademark infringement is probably the least relevant. Here's why.

Trademark law is a branch of consumer protection. Trademark law exists to help consumers distinguish among the various providers of similar goods and services. A trademark indicates the source of goods and services (see Conversation #23).

Over time, trademarks come to represent consumer loyalty and goodwill, and for that reason they become valuable assets to their owners. In trademark infringement cases the parties are typically two businesses claiming the right to use a particular trademark as a trademark: that is, as an indicator of source for their respective goods or services. As an artist (generally) you aren't using the trademark as a trademark. You don't include the Samsonite Corporation's mark in your work because you want to sell luggage. You are depicting the mark in your work for purposes of artistic expression, e.g. there happens to be a Samsonite suitcase in the room you photographed, or you've painted a portrait of a traveler holding a Samsonite product.

The law of trademark infringement has evolved on the assumption that both parties seek to use the disputed mark as a trademark. By and large, therefore, infringement analysis won't apply to your situation.

This is not to say you can never be guilty of trademark infringement when you use a mark in your work. You can. The issue, though, is whether your use of the mark is likely to cause consumer confusion regarding the source of "goods." What goods are we talking about? Your artwork. If the mark appears so prominently in your work, or in such a manner that a reasonable consumer might believe the work was created by or on behalf of the company that owns the mark, there might be a case for trademark infringement. Similarly, if your work is more likely to sell, or to sell at a higher price, solely because it includes the mark, then you're no longer using the mark for purposes of artistic expression. You're trading on the goodwill of the trademark, and that could lead to an infringement action.

Layers #2 and #3: Trade Dress; Right of Publicity. A product's overall packaging and appearance is known as **trade dress**. Trade dress is a type of trademark and can be registered as such, as long as it is sufficiently distinctive and serves no functional purpose. Examples of trade dress include: the shape of a Coca-Cola bottle; the yellow McDonald's arches; the distinctive box for KODAK film. Artists should be aware that trade dress is subject to the same rules regarding use and infringement as are other types of trademarks.

Right of publicity statutes are state laws that protect people (usually famous people) from financial loss when someone uses their likeness, image or identity a.) without permission and b.) for a commercial purpose. Although not technically trademarks, publicity rights are closely related and we often see right of publicity claims joined with trademark claims when Famous Person sues Artist because Artist's work incorporates Famous Person's likeness or identity (see Conversation #25).

Layer #4: First Amendment. Whether you're depicting a trademark or trade dress or the likeness of a famous person, it all comes down to this: do the owner's rights in the mark outweigh your right to free expression? When we're talking about art and trademarks, therefore, the key to everything is the First Amendment to the United States Constitution. Let's look at an example.

New York Racing Assn., Inc. v. *Perlmutter Publishing, et al.* (959 F Supp 578, NDNY 1997). Perlmutter Publishing produced t-shirts that displayed reproductions of certain paintings by Jenness Cortez. Ms. Cortez is a well-known sporting artist whose work depicts the world of thoroughbred horse racing. The paintings in question portrayed the Saratoga Race Course, a thoroughbred flat track in New York State that happens to have a rather unique grandstand. The New York Racing Association (NYRA) operates the Race Course, and contends that Saratoga's grandstand is the second most recognizable structure among racing fans, after the twin spires at Churchill Downs.

> Whether you're depicting a trademark or trade dress or the likeness of a famous person, it all comes down to this: do the owner's rights in the mark outweigh your right to free expression?

Think back to the onion layers we discussed above. NYRA, of course, sued Perlmutter Publishing and Jenness Cortez on grounds of…what? Trade dress. NYRA argued that the grandstand design was "inherently distinctive" (which is the legal test for trade dress protection) and a valuable source of licensing revenue for NYRA and, therefore, that the grandstand image functioned as a trademark for NYRA. NYRA then alleged that Perlmutter's t-shirts infringed on NYRA's rights as owner of the alleged trademark.

It varies from jurisdiction to jurisdiction, but in the Northern District of New York (where this case was decided) a design such as the grandstand is "inherently distinctive," and thus entitled to trade dress protection, only if it serves as an indicator of source. That is, if the owner of the grandstand (NYRA) produced souvenir merchandise akin to what Perlmutter produced: would seeing the grandstand image automatically cause consumers to believe that the merchandise had been produced by NYRA? Stated otherwise, do consumers so associate the grandstand image with NYRA that they assume NYRA to be the source of any and all products depicting that image?

In this case, the court found that NYRA was not entitled to trade dress protection for the grandstand image, and Perlmutter/Cortez prevailed. It is important to note, however, that the court's finding stemmed entirely from NYRA's failure to submit sufficient evidence. Had NYRA submitted samples of its own souvenir merchandise, or other evidence that the grandstand did, in fact, serve as an indicator of source, the result could well have been different.

NYRA also raised claims of trademark infringement because Cortez' work (as reproduced on the t-shirts) contained acknowledged NYRA trademarks (e.g., the NYRA logo) both in the work itself and in the titles of her work. The court again found for Perlmutter/Cortez, holding that NYRA marks in the titles of the work served an artistically relevant purpose: describing the scene depicted in the work. The court balanced NYRA's rights in its marks with Perlmutter/Cortez' rights to free expression and found, on the facts presented, that the need to avoid consumer confusion was negligible as compared to the artist's need to use a trademark in the title of an artistic work. Importantly, the court found this to be so, "regardless of whether the artwork is reproduced on canvas or cotton t-shirts."

With regard to the appearance of NYRA marks in the work itself, the court made an interesting point. Again, it balanced NYRA's rights with those of the artist, and held generally for Perlmutter/Cortez. Where, in real life, the mark actually appears in the scene depicted, the court found that using the mark in art outweighs the need to avoid consumer confusion because it serves the artistically relevant purpose of realism, or accurately depicting the scene. Where, however, the artist simply inserts the mark in the work and, in real life, the mark does not actually appear in the scene, the interest in free expression does not outweigh the need to avoid consumer confusion and an action for trademark infringement could be appropriate.

Where the artist simply inserts the mark in the work and, in real life, the mark does not actually appear in the scene, the interest in free expression does not outweigh the need to avoid consumer confusion and an action for trademark infringement could be appropriate.

In both cases – use of the mark in titles, and use of the mark in the work itself – the court emphasized that its decision was limited to the facts of this particular case. The court observed that NYRA was not nearly as prominent or ubiquitous a mark as, for example, Coca-Cola and that if the NYRA mark had been more prominent the court's analysis might have been different.

The Big Can of Worms: Depicting People in Your Art

Imagine, if you will, the proverbial "can of worms." Pop the top and they're out. Escaping in every direction; impossible to recapture. And the worst part of all? They lurk. They're out there...somewhere. You know the chilling truth: when you least expect it, they're going to return. You will meet again.

MODEL RELEASES

RIGHT TO PRIVACY

RIGHT OF PUBLICITY

WENDT V. HOST INTERNATIONAL

COMMERCIAL SPEECH

FIRST AMENDMENT

HOFFMAN V. CAPITAL CITIES/ABC, INC.

ESTATE OF PRESLEY V. RUSSEN

COMEDY III PRODUCTIONS, INC. V. SADERUP

This conversation examines the tension between an individual's right to control the use of her identity, and an artist's constitutional right to freedom of speech. **When is it OK to use another person's likeness in your work, without first obtaining the subject's consent?**

When you want to use someone's likeness in your work, you need to ask some threshold questions, the most important of which is, **"why the heck don't I just get a release from the subject?"** No kidding. Getting a **release** keeps a lid on this legal can of worms. I heartily recommend the practice.

But if you can't – or didn't – get a release, you and your lawyer will need to conduct a thorough analysis of the situation. You'll need to assess whether the subject is a public figure. You'll need to identify whether the nature of your work is commercial or noncommercial, and you'll need to know how to tell the difference. You may need to consider whether your work is a conventional portrait of the subject, or whether you have added "transformative" artistic elements to the depiction. You'll also need to know that this question raises issues of both state and Federal law and that as to both, a lot depends on the jurisdiction in question. State laws can vary dramatically, as can the Federal courts' analyses on seemingly similar sets of facts.

Using someone's likeness implicates the subject's rights to "privacy" and "publicity," both of which we will examine in a moment. These rights arise under state law. The subject's privacy and publicity rights are balanced by the artist's right to freedom of expression, which arises under the First and Fourteenth Amendments to the United States Constitution.

Let's say you're a professional photographer sitting in an airport coffee shop. You observe a handsome, elderly couple. The wife walks with a cane and the husband (a burly he-man) is carrying a flowery pink cosmetics case. You take a fabulous shot of this couple, right from your perch at the coffee shop. We'll call the couple Mr. and Mrs. Makeup, and for now we will assume that neither is a widely-known "public figure." They do not realize you have taken their photograph, and for some reason you do not run after them waving one of the model release forms you always carry in your camera case.

In general (and please remember this varies from state to state), the **right to privacy** is the right to be free from the publication of embarrassing or private information. Chances are, Mr. Makeup is going to be mighty embarrassed when the boys down at the lodge see your photo of him carrying the pink cosmetics case, especially when it turns out that the woman isn't his wife at all, but his illicit lover. Mr. Makeup is going to sprint to court with a right to privacy claim and you're going to find yourself really wishing you'd gotten that signed release.

Some states recognize a right to privacy only when the subject's likeness has been used in advertising or for a commercial purpose – so how you actually use the photo is an important consideration. Whether you're right or wrong legally, however, is all but immaterial. Once you get sued you incur staggering expense, frustration and damage to your reputation. In short: once you get sued, you lose. Get signed releases and avoid being sued in the first place.

So the right of privacy is basically the right to be free from public embarrassment. What's the difference between the right to privacy and the **right of publicity**? In a word: money.

Let's assume that Mr. Makeup is a famous baseball hero (who didn't take steroids). He's a national icon, a revered public figure. His identity has "commercial value," as evidenced by his numerous endorsement contracts. Whereas privacy laws protect the subject from emotional distress, right of publicity laws protect individuals from the financial loss that occurs when someone uses their likeness without first obtaining a release.

Famous Mr. Makeup could have made money by requiring you to pay a fee for using his likeness in your photograph. When you took the shot and used it without his permission, he lost that potential income. You thus violated Mr. Makeup's right of publicity. George Wendt and John Ratzenberger, the actors who portrayed Norm and Cliff on the TV show, *Cheers,* prevailed on just such a theory when a string of airport taverns introduced life-sized robots modeled on the actors' images.[14]

... how can a celebrity's financial interest trump your constitutional right to freedom of expression? Enter the First Amendment, a.k.a. the big, whopping can of worms.

OK. Mr. Makeup is undeniably famous, there's an applicable right of publicity statute and you do not have a release. But you still want to use that photo! After all, how can a celebrity's financial interest trump your constitutional right to freedom of expression? Enter the First Amendment, a.k.a. the big, whopping can of worms.

Dustin Hoffman brought a right of publicity claim against *L.A. Magazine* when, without the actor's consent, it published an electronically altered version of Mr. Hoffman in his famous pose from the movie, *Tootsie.* Mr. Hoffman prevailed in the lower courts, winning an award in excess of $3 million.[15] On appeal, however, the award was reversed in favor of the magazine's First Amendment defense.[16] *L.A. Magazine* got to use its photo after all, despite California's right of publicity statute. Why? Because the appeals court found the photo was not "commercial speech."

Whether your work (your "speech") is "commercial" or "noncommercial" is, for First Amendment purposes, an extremely complicated legal issue. Debate continues to rage about whether the Hoffman photo was or was not "commercial." The important thing to know, however, is that commercial speech gets less First Amendment protection than noncommercial speech; i.e., it's easier to assert a First Amendment defense if your speech was "noncommercial" than if your speech was "commercial."

In the Hoffman case, once the court determined the photo was entitled to the greater measure of protection accorded to "noncommercial" speech, the only way Mr. Hoffman could defeat *L.A. Magazine's* First Amendment defense was to prove that the magazine acted with "actual malice" in publishing the photo. *New York Times Co.* v. *Sullivan,* 376 U.S. 254, 11 L. Ed. 2d 686, 84 S. Ct. 710 (1964). When Mr. Hoffman was unable to establish actual malice, the magazine's First Amendment rights trumped Mr. Hoffman's claim under California's right of publicity statute.

Balancing individual rights of publicity against an artist's First Amendment rights calls into play many additional factors other than the commercial or noncommercial nature of the artist's work. One such factor is the extent to which the challenged work adds new, "transformative" elements and is not a mere copy or imitation of the subject individual.

Example. The estate of Elvis Presley sued an Elvis impersonator under New Jersey's right of publicity statute.[17] The Presley estate prevailed. Why? Because the court found the impersonator's show simply copied Elvis's act wholesale and served no other socially useful function (e.g., satire, parody, criticism or the dissemination of information.) The impersonator's First Amendment defense thus yielded to Elvis' right of publicity.

Another Example. In California, portrait artist Gary Saderup rendered extremely accurate charcoal drawings of the Three Stooges, and reproduced the drawings as lithographic prints and silkscreened t-shirts. The respective estates of the actors who portrayed the Three Stooges brought a right of publicity claim against Mr. Saderup, and he raised the First Amendment as a defense. The court agreed with Mr. Saderup that his work was expressive, noncommercial speech.[18] The court even included a lengthy discussion about how the right of publicity can frustrate the First Amendment.

> **...commercial speech gets less First Amendment protection than noncommercial speech; i.e., it's easier to assert a First Amendment defense if your speech was "noncommercial" than if your speech was "commercial."**

But then came the clincher. The court held that "literal depiction or imitation" of a celebrity offends California's right of publicity statute and is not protected by the First Amendment unless the work contains "significant transformative elements" (i.e., something to evidence the artist's unique and original artistic message) or the value of the work does not derive primarily from the celebrity's fame. Mr. Saderup's work was so accurate, it caused him to flunk both tests, and the Stooges prevailed.[19]

---

[14] *Wendt* v. *Host International*, 125 F.3d 806 (9th Cir. 1997), cert denied 531 U.S. 811, 148 L. Ed. 2d 13, 121 S. Ct. 33 (2000).

[15] *Hoffman* v.. *Capital Cities/ABC, Inc.*, 33 F. Supp. 2d 867 (C.D. Cal. 1999).

[16] *Hoffman* v. *Capital Cities/ABC, Inc.*, 255 F.3d 1180 (9th Cir. 2001)

[17] *Estate of Presley* v. *Russen*, 513 F. Supp. 1339 (D.N.J.1981)

[18] Just because you sell your work doesn't necessarily mean it's "commercial" (see Conversation #26).

[19] *Comedy III Productions, Inc.* v. *Gary Saderup, Inc*, 25 Cal. 4th 387, 106 Cal. Rptr. 2d 126, 21 P.3d 797, cert denied 534 U.S. 1078, 151 L. Ed. 2d 692, 122 S. Ct. 806 (2002)

Painting Famous Golfers: More on Using People and Trademarks in Your Art

i *f you've depicted somebody else's trademark in your art, your first concern is likely to be trademark infringement. Surprisingly, however, of the legal issues you need to consider, trademark infringement is probably the least relevant.*

ETW CORP. V. JIREH PUBLISHING, INC.

PIRONE V. MACMILLAN, INC.

So we concluded in Conversation #24. A dispute between pro golfer Tiger Woods and sports artist Rick Rush demonstrates why this is so. At issue: may an artist freely create and sell paintings of famous athletes, or must s/he pay for the right to use the athlete's image?

Before discussing the Woods case, let's review some basic concepts.

About trademarks:

• Trademarks exist to indicate the source of goods and services, and as such they help consumers distinguish among the various providers of similar goods and services.

• If you want to protect a mark under United States trademark law you must apply to the United States Patent and Trademark Office (PTO) for a Federal registration. You must apply for registration in one or more of the "classes" that best describe your product or service, e.g., Class 28, Toys and sporting goods; Class 29, Meats and processed foods; Class 41, Education and entertainment, etc.

About Tiger Woods:

• Tiger Woods is famous.

• Because Tiger Woods is famous, his name has commercial value. To protect and exploit that value, Mr. Woods **licenses** the use of his name and image.

• Tiger Woods' given name is Eldrick.

• Mr. Woods created a company to manage the marketing and licensing of his name and image. The company is called "ETW Corp."

Quiz: What do you think ETW stands for?

ETW Corp. filed numerous trademark applications with the PTO for the word mark, "Tiger Woods," and received a Federal registration in Class 16 (Paper Goods and Printed Matter) for, among other things, "art prints" (United States trademark registration number 2194381).

ETW Corp.* v. *Jireh Publishing, Inc., 99 F. Supp. 2d 829, N.D. Ohio [2000]. Rick Rush is an artist from Tuscaloosa, Alabama. For the past 25 years he has been painting famous sports figures in action – many of whom, it bears observing, are more than happy to be featured in his art. Jireh Publishing, Inc. is owned by Mr. Rush's brother, Don, and serves as the exclusive publisher of Mr. Rush's work.

In 1998 Jireh issued a limited edition print of Mr. Rush's, entitled, "The Masters of Augusta." The print depicts Tiger Woods winning the 1997 Masters at Augusta Tournament. Each print sold for $700. Jireh also offered 5,000 lithographs at $15 each. The prints came packaged in a large white envelope bearing the words,

"Masters of Augusta, Tiger Woods." An accompanying insert describes the print as depicting Tiger Woods and "that awesome swing."

ETW brought an action for trademark infringement against Jireh in the United States District Court for the Northern District of Ohio. The court held for Jireh, and its decision was upheld on appeal.[20]

We have already established that,

> [I]n trademark infringement cases the parties are typically two businesses claiming the right to use a particular trademark as a trademark: that is, as an indicator of source for their goods or services. As an artist (generally) you aren't using the trademark as a trademark. You are simply depicting the mark in your work for purposes of artistic expression (Conversation #24).

That's the theory upon which the district court dismissed ETW's claim of trademark infringement. The court stated,

> …it is clear that a plaintiff must show that it has actually used the designation at issue as a trademark, and that the defendant has also used the same or a similar designation as a trademark.

> 99 F. Supp 2d 829, at 833

ETW's problem, in the court's view, was that it had not used the image in question (that is, Mr. Rush's depiction of Tiger Woods) as a trademark. ETW had a Federal registration for the words, "Tiger Woods," but that registration did not extend to the image of Mr. Woods that appeared in Mr. Rush's print. The court analogized ETW's claim to one that Babe Ruth's daughters advanced in *Pirone* v. *MacMillan, Inc.* (894 F. 2d 579, 2d Cir. 1990). In *Pirone,* Ruth's daughters held a registered trademark for the words "Babe Ruth." When MacMillan published a calendar that included three photographs of Babe Ruth, the daughters sued for trademark infringement. The *Pirone* court rejected their claim, stating,

> [plaintiff] would have us read her rights in that word mark [i.e., "Babe Ruth"] to include every photograph of Ruth ever taken. We decline to do so.

Had the Ruth daughters used the specific photographs in question as an indicator of source for particular goods or services, their claim might have prevailed. But they hadn't. Similarly in the ETW case, the district court observed,

> The same is true here where plaintiff [ETW] seems to be asserting that it would have trademark rights in any image or depiction of Tiger Woods even though plaintiff has not shown that it has repeatedly used a single pictorial representation of Tiger Woods as an indicator of origin.

> 99 F. Supp 2d 829, at 833

When you apply for a Federal trademark registration, you can apply just for a "word mark" (such as "Tiger Woods") or you can apply to have a graphic or picture associated with the registration (a "design mark.")

When you apply for a Federal trademark registration, you can apply just for a "word mark" (such as "Tiger Woods") or you can apply to have a graphic or picture associated with the registration (a "design mark.") *Pirone* and the district court's decision in ETW tell us that owning a word mark registration for "Famous Person" won't necessarily afford Famous Person a claim for trademark infringement when Artist creates a visual image of Famous Person in Artist's work. If Famous Person owns a "design mark" registration and Artist uses that design in her work, the case for trademark infringement grows stronger, but Famous Person will still need to prove that Artist was using the design as a trademark and not merely for purposes of artistic expression.

ETW didn't limit its claims against Jireh to trademark infringement. ETW also alleged that Rush's print violated Tiger Woods' **right of publicity** under Ohio state law (see Conversation #25). As we've discussed, rights of publicity vary dramatically from state to state; in general, however, they protect a celebrity's financial interest in the commercial exploitation of his or her identity.

ETW argued that Rush's print was merely "sports merchandise" and not artistic expression, and thus violated Woods' right of publicity. Jireh's position: the print is art, not a commercial exploitation; and as such it is protected by the First Amendment – which trumps the right of publicity.

The court held for Jireh, stating:

...the print at issue herein is an artistic creation seeking to express a message. The fact that it is sold is irrelevant to the determination of whether it receives First Amendment protection.

It's been a long haul for Rick and Don Rush. They vowed to fight until the bitter end, though, because it was the right thing to do. Artists everywhere are glad they did.

---

[20] *ETW Corp.* v. *Jireh Publishing, Inc.*, 99 F. Supp. 2d 829 (N.D. Ohio 2000), affd 332 F.3d 915 (6th Cir. 2003).

Analyzing
Source Material

We set out to take a photograph, compose a symphony, write a play... and the process leads us down paths we'd never imagined. In order to answer Readers' questions for this conversation, I detour from arts law into the scintillating field of grammar.

GRAMMAR

HISTORIC SOURCE
MATERIAL

BUILDINGS AS
TRADEMARKS

TRADEMARK
CLASSES

The dilemma: "historic" or "historical?"

Hmmm.

Wishing to avoid national embarrassment, I scoured the internet until the truth emerged: our rules of grammar are about as clear and predictable as our rules of law. The consensus seems to be that historic refers to someone or something that, itself, is regarded as significant; whereas, historical is something that merely belongs or refers to history. (I also learned, on the very informative website of someone with no credentials whatever, that placing the article "an" before "historic," "historical" or "historian" is widely regarded as nothing short of a pretentious affectation. You be the judge.)

I suppose a roadside marker is historic*al*, unless the marker itself played some part in an extraordinary event. Same with a historic*al* society or museum; same with a work of art that depicts a past era but, itself, played no part in history. That I get. But what about things that are just plain old? Is an unremarkable house that existed during the 1920s histor*ic*, just because it's old?

This conversation involves the extent to which artists may use homes, landmarks and photographs that are... this is my best shot...historic. A Reader from Virginia writes that she lives in a historic town with historic homes and historic landmarks. She would like to photograph and paint these subjects and sell her work in local gift shops as framed art and, on merchandise, as souvenirs for tourists. She asks,

> Would I need special permission from the owners of the homes? Are there complications of which I should be aware?

Another Reader, from Massachusetts, describes himself as an oil painter whose work depicts historic subjects. He writes,

> Though I personally visit and photograph the historic sites for color and landscape reference, I often use photographs found in published text as reference for architectural details. I am uncertain as to whether my paintings are original works of art or are 'derivative' works infringing on the copyright of the published texts and/or the copyright of the historic photos themselves.

Artists can analyze their source material by asking three fundamental questions:

• Is the subject (or source material) protected by copyright law?

• Is the subject (or source material) protected by trademark law?

• Would my depiction of the subject violate anyone's privacy or publicity rights under applicable state law?

Please welcome, once again, our old friends Q and A.

Q: How do I know if my subject or source material is protected by copyright law?

A: In order to answer that question you need to know what types of things copyright protects.

Q: Oh, yeah. What types of things does copyright protect?

A: Weren't you paying attention in Conversation #4? Haven't you memorized Figure 1?

Q *(To self)*: #(*^%(*^*^*#^@^%^#%

Q *(To A)*: Let's say it's a house. That's an architectural work, so it's protected, right?

A: Probably not. Architectural works have only been subject to copyright protection since 1990. If you're talking about a historic building, it was probably created prior to 1990; therefore it's not copyrightable.

Q: What if the landmark is a sculpture?

A: Pictorial, graphic and sculptural works are copyrightable as works of authorship.

Q: So it would be protected, and if I copy it I'm infringing, right?

A: Depends. If it was **published** before 1923 it's in the **public domain** and the copyright protection has expired.

Q: So I have to figure out whether the subject is copyrightable at all, and then if it is, whether the term of copyright protection has yet expired. Right?

A: Right.

Q: Photographs are pictorial works and therefore copyrightable as works of authorship, and so are books. If I copy a photograph from a book, then, am I infringing on two separate copyrights?

A: Possibly. It depends on several factors. Let's assume (because this is usually the case) that the photographer owns the copyright to the photograph that appears in the book. If the photograph is histor*ic* that means it's probably pretty old and the term of copyright has likely expired. If it's historic*al* that means it depicts an earlier era but the photo itself could have been taken any time at all.

Q: Hmm. Grammar makes a difference!

A: Yep.

Q: I need to figure out whether the photo is still under copyright protection, correct?

A: Correct.

Q: And if it is, I'm infringing if I copy it, right?

A: Not necessarily. You're only infringing if you copy protectible elements of the work.

Q: I don't get it.

> Our conversation involves the extent to which artists may use homes, landmarks and photographs that are… this is my best shot…historic.

A: Facts and ideas are not copyrightable (see Conversation #6). Only the original expression of facts and ideas is protectible. If you consult a photograph to ascertain whether a certain vehicle had four windows or six, and you learn it had six, you're not infringing when your own depiction of the vehicle has six windows. If, on the other hand, the photo you consult shows the vehicle against a certain background and with certain lighting – and yours does the same – then you may be infringing on protectible elements of the photographer's original expression.

Q: What about the copyright owner of the book, if I find the photo in a book?

A: We're assuming the photographer owns the copyright to the photo. If the book was written or compiled by someone other than the photographer, the book author has no copyright interest in the photo. The photo is not the author's original expression – it's the photographer's (see Conversation # 4).

Q: Did the book author have to get permission from the photographer to include the photo in the book?

A: Yes. Otherwise the book author would be infringing on the photographer's copyright in the photo.

Q: It sounds like I never have to worry about the copyright of the book – just the photo. Right?

A: Wrong. The book author has copyright rights, too.

Q: In what?

A: In her original expression: original text in the book, page layout, chapter divisions, etc. (see Conversation # 8).

Q: How does that affect me?

A: If you restrict your use to the photo, or material that's not original to the book author, it doesn't. On the other hand, if you copy an entire page of the book and make it the centerpiece of your quilt, then you've infringed on the book author's copyright as well as the photographer's.

Q: Why, again?

If you consult a photograph to ascertain whether a certain vehicle had four windows or six, and you learn it had six, you're not infringing when your own depiction of the vehicle has six windows.

A: Because the book author has a protectible interest in the way that page looks as a whole: its design, captions, sidebar text, etc. Even though the book author lacks a copyright interest in the photo, the author has rights to the manner in which she presented the photo.

> *The conversation suffers from an awkward silence. Momentarily, A reminds Q that in addition to analyzing his source material for copyright issues, he must also consider whether the material is protected by trademark law and/or state laws relating to privacy and publicity. Q thinks A is a colossal pain in the…A…but he knows it's in his own best interest to persevere.*

Q: When I think of trademarks I think of product names, like Tide and Jif. Is that what we're talking about?

A: In part, yes. But trademark law covers more than just words. Designs, shapes, colors, sounds and smells can be trademarks as well.

Q: So a building can be somebody's trademark?

A: It's possible, yes.

Q: How am I supposed to know whether trademark law protects a building or a phrase or something I see in a magazine?

A: Without hiring a lawyer or a professional trademark search firm, you really can't know, for sure. But there are things you can do to make an educated guess.

Q: Like what?

A: First of all, you need to understand what trademark law protects and what it does not protect.

Q *(Settling in for a long winter's nap)*: OK. What does trademark law protect?

A: A trademark identifies the source of particular goods or services. It distinguishes one product (or service) from another. A person or a company acquires trademark rights by actually using the trademark (also known as the "mark") on or in connection with the goods or services the mark identifies.

Q: You know, just once I wish you'd speak English.

A: *Lo siento.* You couldn't get a trademark for, "Tea" if you were using it on…tea. Why? Because that doesn't distinguish your tea from anyone else's. Generic words do not qualify for trademark protection. On the other hand, Lipton is a trademark because it distinguishes Lipton tea from, say, Nestea tea.

Q: So I should ask myself whether images I use in my work identify the source of someone else's goods or services.

A: Exactly.

Q: What do mean, "get" a trademark? You just said a person gets trademark rights by actually using the mark. Do you have to do something else to "get" the trademark?

A: Yes and no. It's a good idea to apply for Federal trademark registration whenever possible because in the event of infringement, the mark owner has broader rights and more opportunities to recover damages. When you see the familiar "®" symbol, that means the mark has a Federal registration. Even if the owner doesn't have a Federal registration, though, he/she/it can still have "common law" rights in a mark. When you see the symbols "TM" or "SM" after a mark, it means that the owner doesn't have a Federal registration, but still intends to protect the mark.

> **When you see the familiar "®" symbol, that means the mark has a Federal registration…. When you see the symbols "TM" or "SM" after a mark, it means that the owner doesn't have a Federal registration, but still intends to protect the mark.**

Q: They can do that?

A: Yes.

Q: What does "SM" mean?

A: Servicemark. It's the same as "TM" (trademark) except it's used in connection with services rather than goods.

Q: So if I see ®, TM or SM it's a signal to me that someone's claiming trademark rights in the mark?

A: Exactly.

Q: And therefore I can't use the mark in my artwork?

A: Not necessarily. You can't use the mark in connection with providing the same goods or services as the owner of the mark, and you can't trade on the goodwill of the mark. But if you're using the mark solely for purposes of artistic expression, chances are you'll be OK (see Conversation # 24). For example, if your source material is a photo and in that photo is a canister of Lipton tea, you aren't infringing on the Lipton mark unless a.) you're using your artwork to sell tea, or b.) the public would be confused into thinking that your work was created by or on behalf of the company that owns Lipton, or c.) your work is more likely to sell, or to sell at a higher price, solely because it includes the mark.

Q: So just because someone holds a trademark doesn't necessarily mean I can't use the mark in my work?

A: That's right. And many trademark holders don't understand this concept. It's very common to encounter trademark holders whose view is, "I own the trademark so you can't use it for anything, no matter what, without paying me." That's simply not true.

Q: Can you give another example?

A: Sure. One of my clients is a photographer. He was hired to photograph the construction process of a new insurance company building. The shape of the new building is very distinctive, and it has come to serve as an indicator of source for the insurance company's services and goodwill. So the insurance company obtained trademark protection for the design of the building – but their protection only extends to the classes in which they applied. Specifically, their classes of protection cover use of the mark (i.e., the building design) in connection with insurance services, and in connection with certain merchandise they distribute to promote the business.

Q: I don't see the problem.

A: Well, my client owns the copyright to his photos, and he makes the photos available for licensing. (Remember, the photos are of the building.) When a textbook company asked to license one of my client's photos for use on the cover of a textbook, the insurance company tried to collect a trademark license fee, citing its trademark registrations for the design of the building.

It's very common to encounter trademark holders whose view is, "I own the trademark so you can't use it for anything, no matter what, without paying me." That's simply not true.

Q: And that was improper?

A: You bet. As I just explained, the insurance company's trademark protection is limited in scope. If the textbook company wanted to use my client's photo to provide insurance services, or similar types of promotional merchandise, then OK – demanding a license would be appropriate. But the insurance company is not in the business of publishing textbooks, and the textbook company has nothing to do with insurance. Furthermore, the textbook company isn't going to sell more books, or sell them for more money, just because a photo of the building appears on the cover.

Q: So it was appropriate for your client to charge a copyright licensing fee, but it was not appropriate for the insurance company to demand a trademark licensing fee.

A: That's right.

Q: Are trademark owners required to use the ®, TM or SM symbols?

A: No.

Q: You mean, someone can be claiming trademark rights to words or a symbol or a design I include in my work, and I might not even know it?

A *(Somewhat sheepishly)*: I'm afraid so. Now that you know how the system works, though, you can at least ask yourself whether it's likely that a particular mark or symbol functions as somebody else's trademark.

Q: Back to that building story. If I used your client's photo to make a giant poster of the building, would I be in trademark trouble with the insurance company?

A: What do you think?

Q (*To self*): I think I hate lawyers.

Q (*To A*): I'd say, "yes," because I'd be trading on the goodwill of the trademarked building design to sell my posters.

A: You're probably right. On the other hand, if you used my client's photo (properly licensed, of course) in your collage reflecting the trends of modern architecture, your use would be for the purpose of artistic expression, and more likely permissible.

Q: Let me switch back to copyright for a minute. What if I used your client's photo and didn't get a copyright license, but I never sold my poster or my collage?

A: Good question. Many artists think it's OK to use copyrighted material as long as they don't sell it. That's not true. If you use protected material without a license, that's infringement even if the work never leaves your basement.

Many artists think it's OK to use copyrighted material as long as they don't sell it. That's not true. If you use protected material without a license, that's infringement even if the work never leaves your basement.

Q: OK. Back to trademark. How else can I determine whether someone's claiming rights to a particular mark?

A: As I said before, to be absolutely certain you must seek professional advice. You can do a preliminary search yourself, though, on the website of the United States Patent and Trademark Office: http://www.uspto.gov/main/trademarks.htm

Q: Can you register trademarks with the states, as well as Federally?

A: Yes.

Q: Is there any particular symbol that serves as an indicator of state registration?

A: You're starting to sound like a lawyer.

Q: Very funny. What's the answer?

A: No. TM and SM are general indicators that a mark owner is hoping to preserve all rights in the mark – including those arising under state law.

Q: Hey. If trademark rights are as limited as you say, why can McDonald's stop almost anyone from using the golden arches or the prefix "Mc...." ?

A: There are exceptions for marks that have become really famous.

Q: (*Speechless*): ??

A: Listen, it's been a long day and you still need to think about whether using your source material will violate anyone's privacy or publicity rights under state law.

Q: I'll just re-read Conversations #24, #25 and #26.

A: Good idea. You can also check out the Library of Congress' explanation at: http://lcweb2.loc.gov/ammem/copothr.html

Your Business

Art on Consignment: Gallery Creditors

What happens to my art if it's hanging in a restaurant and the restaurant goes bankrupt?

To address that question, I need to change it. This is called, "framing the issue." (There's a joke there since we're talking about art, but it's so obvious I'd just embarrass myself by pursuing it.)

The issue, really, is this: Can a gallery's creditors seize art that's being held on consignment?

The answer is yes.

You: *Horrified,* "Yes?"

In a worst case scenario, yes. It surprises many (including lawyers) to learn that a gallery's creditors can seize **consignment** pieces and/or the proceeds from such pieces, even though title to the art never passed to the gallery.

Happily, there are ways to protect against this odious consequence. Some states (but not all) have pro-artist consignment laws that shield the art from a gallery's creditors. And in most states without art consignment laws, there are affirmative steps artists can (and must) take to protect themselves.

If you're going to sell work on consignment, there is absolutely no alternative: you must be familiar with the law that applies in your jurisdiction.

The first thing to do is find out if your state has a "consignment law" that applies specifically to art and artists. The following website offers links to the laws of most US states: http://www.law.cornell.edu/states/listing.html

Click on your state, then click on "Statutes." That will take you to your state's legislative website. Most state sites offer a user-friendly search function. Enter a few good keywords and within seconds you'll have a list of relevant statutes. I tried a few states at random and had the best luck when I used keywords such as "artist," "art," "dealer" and "consignment" in various combinations.

If your state's site does not have a search function, you'll probably need to consult an attorney to find out whether your state has an art consignment law. (Note to New Yorkers: your website's search function is useless unless you already know the section you're looking for, so head in the direction of Arts and Cultural Affairs Law sections 11 and 12.) There are books you can consult on this topic, but remember that the law changes constantly – and these books become outdated very quickly. It's better practice to consult an official source with the most up-to-date version of your state's statutes. If doing so is not within your interests or abilities, hire a lawyer to do it for you. It won't take an attorney very long to find the law, and this is well worth the investment.

If your state has an art consignment law, read it carefully, because consignment laws vary considerably from state to state. As a threshold matter, you and your attorney will want to clarify whether the law applies to you at all, based on your statute's definitions of "art," "artist" and "consignment."

What if your state either doesn't have a consignment law, or it doesn't apply to you, or its provisions don't cover your particular set of facts?

Then you need to find out whether your state has adopted a version of the Uniform Commercial Code, or "UCC." (Typically this is pronounced "you-see-see," though I suppose you could also make it rhyme with "yuck.") Back in 1892 the American Bar Association (ABA) recognized that sometimes it's valuable to have uniformity among state laws. The ABA thus convened the first National Conference of Commissioners on Uniform State Laws (NCCUSL) which set to work drafting "uniform" laws on various topics which states were then encouraged (but not required) to adopt. NCCUSL continues its work today; you can learn more at: http://www.nccusl.org/Update/

Most states have adopted some version of the UCC, governing commercial transactions. Unless you live in Louisiana, you can find a link to your state's version at: http://www.law.cornell.edu/uniform/ucc.html

UCC Article 2 covers the sale of goods, and consignment relationships. Chances are your state does have a version of UCC Article 2, and that, in the absence of an applicable art consignment law, its provisions will govern when a gallery's creditors attempt to seize your art. This is not good news!

The UCC favors good faith creditors. Our first clue in this regard is the caption of the applicable provision, UCC §2-326: "Consignment Sales and Rights of Creditors." Section 2-326 defines two categories of transactions in which the "buyer" can return goods to the "seller." The transaction is a "sale or return" if the goods are delivered primarily for resale. The transaction is a "sale on approval" if the goods are delivered primarily for the buyer's own use.

If you're going to sell work on consignment, there is absolutely no alternative: you must be familiar with the law that applies in your jurisdiction.

Let's pause for clarification. In an artist-gallery consignment situation, the "buyer" is the gallery and the "seller" is the artist. The gallery is also known as the "consignee" and the artist is the "consignor." So:

Gallery = buyer, consignee

Artist = seller, consignor

When an artist delivers art to a gallery "on consignment," the idea is for the gallery to sell the art to a third party. Consequently, since the "goods" (i.e., the pieces of art) were delivered primarily for resale, the transaction is a "sale or return" transaction rather than a "sale on approval" transaction. This is where things turn nasty, because UCC §2-326(2) states that although goods held "on approval" are not subject to the claims of the buyer's (i.e., the gallery's) creditors, goods held on "sale or return" are subject to such claims while they are in the buyer's possession.

The UCC provides three ways to protect one's art from claims of the gallery's creditors. The first method only works in states that have "sign laws" (and not too many states have them). If your state happens to have a sign law, you can insist that the gallery position a sign by your art, placing the world on notice that the art is being held on consignment and that you, the consignor, have a superior interest in it.

Under the second method, you can protect your work by establishing that the person conducting the business (i.e., the gallery) "is generally known by his creditors to be substantially engaged in selling the goods of others." This means you'll have to prove (probably in court) that the gallery's creditors actually knew that the gallery regularly sold consignment work rather than work the gallery owned outright. It's something of a crapshoot as to whether you'll be successful in meeting your burden of proof. If the "gallery" is a restaurant, for example, the restaurant is probably not known to its creditors as being substantially engaged in the business of selling the goods (artwork) of others. This method, therefore, is far from foolproof.

The third method is much more reliable, but it's difficult and complicated. To protect your work under the third method, you need to file a **security interest** in the art. You do this (or more accurately, your attorney does this) by complying with your state's version of UCC Article 9.

And that's it. If there's no consignment statute you either have a sign law (and use it); or you gamble on meeting the burden of proof; or you hire an attorney to file a security interest under UCC Article 9.

OK. You've protected your art from the gallery's creditors. Now what happens if the gallery burns down with your work inside?

Read on.

Art on Consignment:
Who Bears the Risk of Loss?

gallery offering to represent me sent a contract with the following clause:

"The Gallery assumes no responsibility for any consigned work lost, stolen or damaged while in the Gallery's possession."

....

INSURANCE
STRICT LIABILITY
BAILMENT

I have three other galleries representing me, and this is the first time I've encountered such a clause. When asked, this is how the gallery owner replied:

"Insurance costs have skyrocketed since 9/11. We are one of many galleries that no longer assume any liability for work left at the gallery. Most artists who have been exhibiting a long time are used to this. As an emerging artist you need to weigh showing your work at your own risk or not showing it. The decision is yours."

Are insurance responsibilities, once borne by galleries, now falling to artists?

The insurance climate has changed dramatically since the events of September 11, 2001, causing artists and galleries alike to feel the crunch of soaring premiums. Because galleries need to cut costs like everyone else, this gallery owner's take-it-or-leave-it approach is not surprising. But is it legal?

It depends on where you live.

As we discussed in Conversation #28, many states have laws governing consignment and the artist-gallery relationship. The issue at hand – whether a gallery can disclaim all liability for art left at the gallery – similarly requires analysis under individual state consignment statutes.

Let's assume that your state does, indeed, have an art consignment statute. What does that mean in terms of gallery liability? The answer lies in the text of the statute. Here, for example, is Alaska's provision:

(a) When an artist delivers or causes to be delivered a work of art of the artist's own creation to an art dealer for the purpose of sale, or exhibition and sale, on a commission, fee, or other basis of compensation, the acceptance of the work of art by the art dealer is a consignment, and

(1) the art dealer is, with respect to the work of art, the agent of the artist;

(2) the work of art is trust property in the hands of the art dealer for the benefit of the artist;

(3) proceeds from the sale of the work of art are trust funds in the hands of the art dealer for the benefit of the artist;

(4) the art dealer shall return an unsold work of art on demand of the artist;

(5) the art dealer is strictly liable for loss or damage to a work of art while the work of art is in the possession of the art dealer; the value of a lost or damaged work of art is the value established by written agreement between the artist and art dealer before the loss or damage of the work of art; if no written agreement establishing the value of the work of art exists, the value is the fair

market value of the work of art less the art dealer's commission or fee….

Alaska Statutes §45.65.200.

Think back to the gallery owner at the top of this conversation. If the gallery's in Alaska, the owner is strictly liable for loss or damage to art in the gallery's possession and the "take-it-or-leave-it" position she so confidently espoused to the artist is illegal and unenforceable.

Or is it?

As it turns out, Alaska has another statute that allows artists to waive their protections:

> *A provision of a contract or agreement whereby the artist waives a provision of AS 45.65.200 is void except as provided in this subsection. An artist may waive the provisions of AS 45.65.200 if the waiver is clear, conspicuous, and agreed to in writing by the artist….*

Alaska Statutes § 45.65.210.

The Alaskan gallery owner can present the artist with "take-it-or-leave-it" after all: either sign this clear, conspicuous waiver saying my gallery has no liability, or don't exhibit your work.

Wisconsin has a provision similar to Alaska's:

> *The art dealer is strictly liable for the loss of or damage to the work of fine art while it is in the art dealer's possession….*

Wisconsin Statutes § 129.02(4).

In Wisconsin, however, the corresponding waiver statute is short and sweet (for the artist):

> *Waiver voided. Any portion of an agreement which waives any provision of this chapter is void.*

Wisconsin Statutes § 129.07.

In Wisconsin, then, a "take-it-or-leave-it" waiver won't fly. The gallery's liable, period. Here, of course, is where the artist needs to be savvy about his rights. If a Wisconsin artist didn't know about the "no waiver" law, the artist might sign an unscrupulous gallery's "take-it-or-leave-it" waiver not realizing it's absolutely void. Similarly, in Alaska, an unsuspecting artist might not realize that unless the artists has signed a waiver the gallery is, in fact, strictly liable for the art.

The insurance climate has changed dramatically since the events of September 11, 2001, causing artists and galleries alike to feel the crunch of soaring premiums.

Other states have lesser measures of protection. In Maryland, art on consignment is **bailment** property in the hands of the gallery (Maryland Statutes §11-8A-02). Bailment is a legal term referring to the standard of care one party must exercise when lawfully holding the property of another. In general, bailment imposes less liability on a gallery than, for example, the strict liability standard found in the Alaska and Wisconsin statutes. Minnesota's standard is vaguer still. In that state a gallery "*is responsible for* the loss of, or damage to the work of art" held on consignment (Minnesota Statutes §324.03). Just how far the gallery's liability extends, we can't tell from the face of the Minnesota statute.

The point, of course, is that you need to know the law of your jurisdiction. The gallery owner our Reader described, above, may have been totally within her rights to disclaim all liability for the artist's art. Or, depending on the jurisdiction, her disclaimer could have been flat-out illegal, and advancing it nothing more than a smokescreen.

If your state does not have consignment laws, or if your laws do not impose liability upon the galleries, the game isn't necessarily over. Re-visit Conversation #28, and think about the Uniform Commercial Code. In addition to governing the rights of creditors, most states' versions of the UCC also address liability for damage to consigned goods. Artists should explore this avenue before submitting blindly to a gallery's waiver of liability.

Even though galleries can be held liable – sometimes – for damage to your work, you still need to be insured. Artists should take care to obtain coverage for their work while it's still in the studio, while it's in transit and, if necessary, while it's on display. If the work itself could cause injury to others, liability insurance for that purpose is also a good idea. For a list of insurance resources, just enter the phrase "art insurance" into any major search engine.

Buy-Sell Agreements

do you run a gallery with others? Do you hold an ownership interest in any other type of business? If so, it's important to ensure that when ownership interests in the business are transferred – as they inevitably will be – they pass back to your company and/or to individuals with whom you know you can do business. Buy-sell agreements are the way to make this happen. Whether your company is a mighty corporation or a simple partnership, overlooking the importance of a buy-sell agreement can be a tragic, expensive mistake.

....

BUSINESS ENTITY FORMATION

LIMITED LIABILITY COMPANIES

FUNDING BUY-SELL AGREEMENTS

BUSINESS VALUATION

Ann, Bridget and Chuck (not their real names) are all visual artists. They retained me to create a business entity through which they would open a gallery to display and sell their own work and the juried work of other artists. At first they wanted to organize as a non-profit corporation and seek **tax-exempt** status. I advised against this because their primary objectives were neither charitable nor educational and the likelihood of obtaining tax-exempt status was slim (see Conversation #32).

These artists wanted to sell art. Period. That's a for-profit business endeavor. In terms of choosing an appropriate business entity, therefore, A, B and C could organize as a **partnership**, a **business corporation** or a **limited liability company** (LLC). Generally speaking (and there are always exceptions) a partnership offers favorable income tax treatment but exposes the partners to risks of personal liability. A corporation offers liability protection, but often results in double taxation treatment for its **shareholders**. An LLC provides the best of both for its members: the favorable tax treatment of a partnership plus the liability protection of a corporation. A, B and C chose the LLC.

(I stray from the conversation for just a moment to offer the following words of caution. The cost of creating and maintaining an LLC varies from state to state. My Wisconsin clients pay the state $130 to form the LLC and $25 per year thereafter. My New York clients pay the state $200 to form the LLC and $100 per member thereafter, every fiscal year. If Ann, Bridget and Chuck formed their LLC in Wisconsin they'd pay the state $130 plus $25 per year. In New York they'd pay the state $200 plus $300 per year. Know what you're getting into before indiscriminately forming an LLC or any other type of business entity.)

So I formed the LLC. At that point, Ann, Bridget and Chuck were all **members** of the LLC. Each made an initial contribution to the company (called their "capital contributions"), determining the percentage of their membership interests. Let's say that Ann contributed cash, Bridget contributed more cash and Chuck contributed services but no cash. The members agreed (in their **operating agreement**) that the value of Chuck's services was equal to the amount of cash that Ann contributed. All told, Ann and Chuck each held a 30% interest in the LLC, and Bridget held a 40% interest.

They thought everything was settled until I started asking a few questions:

What happens when Ann wants to retire?

What happens if Chuck becomes disabled?

What happens if Bridget goes bankrupt?

Art's Gallery

OPEN

What happens if Chuck gets divorced?

What happens when the Members die?

Horrific possibilities started to form in their minds. In the absence of a **buy-sell agreement** any of the members could simply transfer their membership interests in the company to anyone they wished: Ann could sell out to a random purchaser; Bridget could transfer her interest to a trustee in bankruptcy; Chuck's interest could be awarded to his former spouse; any of the members' interests could pass to heirs upon their deaths. Should such transfers occur, the remaining members would find themselves in business with strangers. Imagine the fun Ann and Bridget would have sharing the gallery with Chuck's former wife. Or suppose Bridget died and her good-for-nothing nephew inherited her controlling interest in the company. Yikes!

A buy-sell agreement is a contract among those with ownership interests in a business. It can be a stand-alone contract or it can be part of the business' governing documents, e.g., part of an LLC's operating agreement; part of a partnership agreement; part of the **by-laws** of a corporation. Where the agreement resides is far less important than the fact that it does, in fact, exist.

Buy-sell agreements can determine, in advance of controversy, **when** an owner may sell his or her interest in the business; **who** may purchase the interest; **what** price will be paid for the interest; and **how** the seller of the interest will be paid. A little effort up front can save a whole lot of grief down the road.

Structuring the buy-sell agreement is not a do-it-yourself task. Not even for me. Buy-sell agreements have significant income and estate tax implications for those with ownership interests in the business. A critical player in this process, therefore, is your accountant or tax specialist. Ideally you should retain an attorney and an accountant, both of whom are familiar with your business and with the individual owners, and the accountant and attorney should consult with one another as your buy-sell agreement is being developed.

> **A buy-sell agreement is a contract among those with ownership interests in a business. It can be a stand-alone contract or it can be part of the business' governing documents**

There are two basic ways that buy-sell agreements can be structured. In the first, the company itself buys the departing owner's interest. (This is called an **entity-purchase buyback**). In the second, the remaining owners purchase the departing owner's interest. (This is called a **cross-purchase buyback**). Either way, strangers are effectively prevented from acquiring ownership interests in the business.

Let's go back to Ann, Bridget and Chuck. I drafted their LLC operating agreement to include buy-sell provisions. Chuck, whose contributions to the gallery consist entirely of services, noticed that the new buy-sell provisions authorized the company first, and if the company passed then Ann and Bridget, to purchase his membership interest in the event he became totally disabled. Chuck had no objection to this, but he wondered how either the company, or Ann or Bridget individually, would be able to afford the purchase, should his disability occur.

The answer: disability insurance. The LLC and/or Ann and Bridget personally, could take out disability insurance on Chuck. Then, in the event of his disability, the insurance proceeds would provide funds for purchasing his membership interest. Similarly, the company and/or the individual members could take out life insurance on the lives of the other members and, in the event of death, the proceeds would provide funds for purchasing the deceased member's interest.

Insurance works for death and disability, but not for other transfer events such as retirement, discord, divorce or bankruptcy. In those cases the LLC and individual members would need to pursue alternative financing options such as borrowing and installment payment plans. Good old fashioned saving is another way to prepare for a buy-sell event, though corporations need to be wary because they can only pile up so much undistributed income before getting taxed on excess reserves. An important thing to remember is that most states require organized business entities to remain solvent after a buy-sell event. Buying out the departing owner's interest, in other words, can't bankrupt the company.

Another important part of the buy-sell agreement is valuation. One way or another, the agreement needs to specify either a fixed dollar amount for each owner's interest, or a formula for determining such values. And the valuation needs to be reasonable. If Ann, Bridget and Chuck fixed the value of each member's interest at $5.00 and the company made millions in profits, the IRS would frown. Actually the IRS would bellow and A, B & C would be made to suffer. So don't undervalue or overvalue your ownership interests, and obtain advice on this issue from a good accountant or business valuation specialist before finalizing your buy-sell agreement.

Blue Shirt:
Anatomy of a Commissioning Agreement

Several years ago the county of Milwaukee, Wisconsin invited proposals for a large-scale sculpture to be installed in a new parking structure at Mitchell International Airport. The county oversees the airport and pays for airport improvements by collecting user fees from the airlines. Money from airline user fees was slated to pay for the sculpture.

PUBLIC ART

COMMISSIONING
AGREEMENTS

CONTRACTS
(BREACH)

Approximately 100 artists submitted proposals, and in 2001 a panel of community leaders tapped Dennis Oppenheim for the Mitchell project. Mr. Oppenheim presented the panel with two alternative concepts: *Blue Shirt*, a 2-story, 30' x 40' translucent shirt that would encompass an entire side of the parking structure and feature a floor with furniture reflecting the human physiology; and *Leaving Home*, a long, twisted sculpture depicting a bus that would wind its way down the side of the building. The panel chose *Blue Shirt*.

Mr. Oppenheim and the county entered into a commissioning contract, agreeing that *Blue Shirt* would be completed and installed by the spring of 2002. The county adjusted that date, however, when it became apparent that the parking structure itself would not be completed within the original timeframe. Mr. Oppenheim's deadline for *Blue Shirt* was pushed back to January 31, 2003.

In the meantime, the county had a change in leadership. The County Executive in power during the artist selection phase (Mr. A), was an enthusiastic supporter of *Blue Shirt*. Sometime in 2002, however, Mr. B succeeded Mr. A as County Executive. Mr. B made no secret of his distaste for the *Blue Shirt* project. Mr. B and other detractors contended that the sculpture was a slur on Milwaukee's blue-collar heritage; they also felt it was "awkward" for the site. Undoubtedly, the project's price tag was an additional concern.

According to Mr. Oppenheim, extending the installation deadline to January 2003 put him behind schedule because, among other things, he had to find a different company to fabricate materials for the project. He cited additional factors, as well. For whatever reason(s), Mr. Oppenheim missed the January 31 deadline and, as they say in circles more genteel than my own, "all heck broke loose."

In early February (scant hours after the January 31 deadline) Mr. B announced that the county was going to cancel the commission and ditch *Blue Shirt* altogether, because Mr. Oppenheim had missed the deadline. Even considering Mr. B's outspoken opposition to the project, this was a surprising move. The county had already paid Mr. Oppenheim $165,000 on his $220,000 contract, and from that Mr. Oppenheim had paid $80,000 to the company he'd selected to build the sculpture.

How could Mr. B do this? Isn't a contract a contract?

Let's look at some of the major contract issues in the *Blue Shirt* controversy. First, though, a caveat: contract law varies from state to state, and there is no substitute for being familiar with the law of the jurisdiction that controls your contract (see Conversation #28). The concepts that follow are general principles that may or may not apply in your jurisdiction.

Have a written contract. The county and Mr. Oppenheim had, in fact, executed a written commissioning contract before Mr. Oppenheim began his work. This is one of the few things that "went right" in the whole *Blue Shirt* debacle. It is essential to have a written contract in place before work commences on an artistic commission. Key issues to be addressed in such a contract include (and this is not an exhaustive list):

- a recital of the facts underlying the agreement;

- a detailed description of the work to be created, and its title;

- the amount of the artist's compensation, the mode of payment and a timetable for payment;

- resolution of all intellectual property issues (copyright, trademark, patent, trade secrets);

- provisions addressing maintenance and future ownership of the work;

- timelines and warranties;

- definitions of terms;

- dispute resolution provisions;

- "governing law" and other "miscellaneous" provisions.

Time is of the essence. In general, if it's really important that the other side perform its contractual obligations precisely on the date(s) specified in the contract, it's best to include a clause stating that "time is of the essence." If there is no such clause and there's no indication that one party has been substantially harmed by the other party's delay, courts are likely to apply the rule of reason and excuse minor delays. That is to say, a minor delay by the other side will not be your ticket to getting out of the contract and recovering vast sums in damages.

Material (as opposed to technical) breach of contract. It is important for commissioning contracts to specify what acts or omissions will be considered material breaches of the contract. A **material breach** is one that's so significant, and so harmful to the other party, that it excuses performance by the nonbreaching party. In other words, if a court found that Mr. Oppenheim's failure to meet the January 31 deadline caused such hardship to the county that it rose to the level of a material breach, then the county might have been justified in canceling the contract and failing to perform its remaining contractual obligations. On the other hand, if the court found that failing to meet the January 31 deadline was not terribly significant and did little to harm the county, then it would have been deemed a **technical breach**, and would not have provided the county with a legal basis for getting out of the contract.

The allure of winning a lucrative, high profile public commission can be intoxicating. The reality of politics and bureaucracy can be so emotionally and financially costly, however, that dealing with government might or might not be worth it.

Good faith goes a long way. The parties to a contract have an obligation to act in good faith. They are expected to act in the best interest of accomplishing the goal(s) of the agreement, and not to take advantage of one another by invoking legal technicalities. The party that can demonstrate good faith has a significant advantage in court. Mr. Oppenheim made numerous overtures to the county to meet and negotiate and work out their differences. That's good faith. If media reports are correct, the county appears to have rejected Mr. Oppenheim's overtures. That's not good faith; nor is pouncing on a missed deadline hours after it passes – particularly when you yourself may partially be at fault for the failure.

Know the political climate. The allure of winning a lucrative, high profile public commission can be intoxicating. The reality of politics and bureaucracy can be so emotionally and financially costly, however, that dealing with government might or might not be worth it:

• Will zoning be a consideration? Know the code, inside and out.

• Are elections coming up? Think about how changes in leadership could affect your working relationship.

• Is your work likely to be controversial? Develop a public relations strategy to pave the way. (Many believe that canceling Mr. Oppenheim's contract was akin to censorship, thinly veiled beneath dubious claims to breach of contract.)

Bottom line: make sure you enter into publicly funded projects with your eyes wide open and your contracts well prepared.

Eye on Nonprofits

Warning: the following scenario may prove heartbreaking for sensitive Readers.

A group of artists decides to form a "nonprofit." The artists can barely contain their excitement for the projects they're going to sponsor, the artwork they're going to sell and the people they're going to serve. They hold a bake sale and raise $75, and then they come to see me. Eyes wide and extending the $75 (in a plastic bag filled with dimes and quarters), the leader explains, "We'd like you to fill out the form so we can get our 501(c) (3)." My heart sinks. Yet again, I'm the one who has to break the news about Santa Claus.

....

FORMING A NONPROFIT CORPORATION

STEPS FOR OBTAINING FEDERAL TAX-EXEMPT STATUS

The term, "501(c) (3)" is tossed about rather freely. It's become a noun (as in, "we're getting our 501[c] [3]" and "they're a 501[c][3]"). Most unfortunately, it has become a designation to which many organizations consider themselves unconditionally entitled. Some, like the artists above, have sincerely noble intentions. Others seek 501(c)(3) status to avoid paying income tax. Either way, the prevailing notion is that all one needs to do is fill out a form and ... *voila!*... you're a 501(c)(3). Not so.

"501(c)(3)" refers to section 501, subdivision (c)(3) of the **Internal Revenue Code**. Organizations existing for the purposes set forth in subdivision (c)(3) qualify for Federal tax-exempt status, and with certain restrictions donations to such organizations are tax-deductible to the donors. What many people don't realize is that section 501(c) has 27 subdivisions other than (c)(3), each requiring totally different criteria for qualification (see IRS Publication 557, pages 60-61; http://www.irs.gov/pub/irs-pdf/p557.pdf). Consequently, any organization applying to the IRS for tax-exempt status must first identify the appropriate subdivision of section 501(c) under which to apply. The appropriate subdivision might or might not be subdivision (c)(3), depending on the primary purposes and activities of the organization.

Section 501(c) (3) applies exclusively to organizations that exist for *religious, educational, charitable, scientific or literary purposes*; that *provide testing for public safety*; or that exist *to foster national or international amateur sports competition and/or the prevention of cruelty to children or animals.*

Once again, our friends Q and A.

A: What's wrong with this picture?

Q: The term "artistic" does not appear anywhere on that list of qualifying purposes.

A. Very good.

Q: So how does an arts organization acquire 501(c) (3) status?

A: It must demonstrate that although its activities are artistic in nature, the organization nonetheless exists for one or more of the purposes that do appear on the list.

Q: Then, for musical and visual arts organizations it must be even harder to obtain 501(c) (3) status than it is for organizations whose primary activities correspond directly with the purposes set forth in subdivision (c)(3).

A. Exactly.

The application process for obtaining 501(c)(3) status is formidable, and I won't pull any punches. Your group needs to exist – in a well-organized manner – for at least a year before you even think about applying for 501(c)(3) status. This is not a legal requirement; it's just my view. But I firmly believe it, and here's why.

First, you need to devote a substantial amount of time to something most would-be nonprofits ignore: selecting your name. Is the domain name available? Increasingly, an organization's website is its lifeblood. If you invest time and money in a name for which you cannot obtain an identical or intuitively similar domain name, you're at a disadvantage. More critically, you need to make sure that neither your organizational name nor your domain name is somebody else's trademark. Getting sued for trademark infringement is a poor way to commence your nonprofit existence.

You need to incorporate in your state. I'll use New York as an example; you must get individualized advice regarding proper procedure for incorporating in your own state. In New York, there are four different types of nonprofit corporations: Types A, B, C and D (and who said New Yorkers aren't creative?) You need to identify which type you are. Then you need to draft your corporate purposes. Doing this properly is enormously important, because when ultimately you apply for 501(c)(3) status, the IRS will very closely examine your organization's stated purposes.

Do not make the mistake of filling your board with artists. Your organization is as much a business as the local widget factory, and your board must include professionals from all walks of business life. In my opinion your first recruit should always be an accountant.

Do you anticipate that your organization will ever own real property? In New York you'll want to know about specific language that will help you acquire property tax exemption when the time comes.

You must select the prescribed number of individuals to serve as your initial directors and you must draft, finalize and notarize your certificate of incorporation. In New York most cultural organizations need to have their certificates of incorporation approved by the State Education Department – so if you skip that step your application for incorporation will be rejected.

Once you've submitted the application for incorporation it's time to recruit your full board of directors. Do not make the mistake of filling your board with artists. Your organization is as much a business as the local widget factory, and your board must include professionals from all walks of business life. In my opinion your first recruit should always be an accountant. When the IRS is scrutinizing your 501(c) (3) application, your organization's financial house must be in order. Make it clear to the accountant on your board that his or her job is to make sure the board establishes sound financial policies for the organization and that staff properly implements those policies on a daily basis.

Continue board development by recruiting representatives from your community's primary employers, persons skilled in your organizational mission, an attorney skilled in nonprofit and arts law (the personal injury lawyer doesn't do much good), and of course – some heavy hitting philanthropists (see http://www.directorconnector.com)

When recruiting is complete, hold your first board meeting. At that meeting you will elect officers of the board, adopt by-laws, adopt your mission and vision statements, adopt board policies and map out your fundraising plan. If that sounds like a tall order, it is. But if you don't do all those things – competently – you won't obtain 501(c)(3) status.

After the state confers corporate status, you must obtain an **Employer Identification Number** (EIN) for the organization, and open a bank account using the EIN. Don't forget to establish board policies regarding check-signing procedures, and pay close attention to your budget: it's got to be detailed and realistic. Establish your accounting, financial and internal control systems; analyze and execute your staffing and volunteer needs; set up a reliable record-keeping system. Analyze your insurance needs in areas such as workers' compensation, unemployment, disability, general property and liability, auto liability and directors and officers' liability. How are those finances coming along? You need accurate income and expense forecasts for at least two years. Have you secured your office space and necessary equipment? Do you have a reliable gift receipt system?

Remember, although you may now be a nonprofit corporation in the eyes of your state, you do not yet have Federal tax-exempt status. (That's the difference between **nonprofit** and **tax exempt**.) At this point donations to your organization are not tax-deductible to the donors, and you do have to pay Federal income tax.

In most states, being a nonprofit corporation means having to file a lot of reports. Make sure you've got systems in place to ensure these reports get filed accurately and on time.

Remember, although you may now be a nonprofit corporation in the eyes of your state, you do not yet have Federal tax-exempt status.

Now – and only now – you might be ready to apply for 501(c)(3) status. And trust me; applying for tax-exempt status requires a whole lot more than just filling out a form. You need a track record, proving that you have successfully accomplished the items I've outlined above. You need concrete examples of services you've provided, consistent with the corporate purposes set forth in your articles of incorporation and by-laws. You must demonstrate that volunteers contribute in meaningful ways to the organization's mission and that you have significant expectations of public support. You'll be asked to write detailed narratives, and to submit financial records and realistic projected budgets. In short, you've got to be a real business with your "act" entirely together.

The benefits of 501(c)(3) status are significant and if your organization realistically has a chance of qualifying for such status, go for it. Do so, however, not as a wide-eyed innocent, but rather as an informed businessperson with eyes wide open.

Online Resources

The Advertising Council...http://www.adcouncil.org/

Basic Facts About Patents...http://www.uspto.gov/main/patents.htm

Copyright Law: Section 101 definitions ....http://www.copyright.gov/title17/92chap1.html#101

Copyright Law: Section 106 bundle of rights ....http://www.copyright.gov/title17/92chap1.html#106

Copyright Office: Circular 3 (copyright notice).............................http://www.copyright.gov/circs/circ03.pdf

Copyright Office: Circular 14 (derivative works) http://www.copyright.gov/circs/circ14.pdf

Copyright Office: Circular 15a (copyright duration)...................http://www.copyright.gov/circs/circ15a.pdf

Copyright Office: Circular 31 (ideas, methods or systems)...........http://www.copyright.gov/circs/circ31.pdf

Copyright Office: Circular 34 (names, titles, short phrases) http://www.copyright.gov/circs/circ34.pdf

Copyright Office: Circular 38a (international treaties)................http://www.copyright.gov/circs/circ38a.pdf

Copyright Office: Circular 40
   (copyright registration, works of visual art) http://www.copyright.gov/circs/circ40.pdf

Copyright Office: Circular 41 (architectural works)......................http://www.copyright.gov/circs/circ41.pdf

Copyright Office: Circular 44
   (cartoons, comic strips, characters)...http://www.copyright.gov/circs/circ44.pdf

Copyright Office: Circular 65
   (copyright registration, automated databases).........................http://www.copyright.gov/circs/circ65.pdf

Copyright Office: Circular 66
   (copyright registration, online works) http://www.copyright.gov/circs/circ66.pdf

Copyright Office: FL-102 (fair use) http://www.copyright.gov/fls/fl102.pdf

Copyright Office: FL-103 (useful articles) http://www.copyright.gov/fls/fl103.pdf

Copyright Office: FL-115
   (copyright registration, works of visual art)....................................http://www.copyright.gov/fls/fl115.pdf

Copyright Office: FL-124
   (group registration of published photographs) http://www.copyright.gov/fls/fl124.pdf

Cornell Legal Information Institute:
   links to state and Federal statutes...http://www.law.cornell.edu/statutes.html

Acceptance In contract law, words or actions signifying consent to the terms of an offer.

Actual damages In litigation, an amount awarded to the prevailing party for his/her actual, out-of-pocket loss or injury (as opposed to "special" or "statutory" damages, which typically exceed the party's actual losses).

Alternative dispute resolution Methods, other than litigation in the public courts, by which conflicts and disputes are resolved privately. ADR usually takes one of two forms: mediation or arbitration. It typically involves a process much less formal than the traditional court process and includes the appointment of a third-party to preside over a hearing between the parties. ADR is quicker and less expensive than court litigation. Usually, however, it does require compromise.

Art executor An entity or individual appointed in one's will specifically for the purpose of managing that part of an artist's or collector's estate that consists of artwork. An art executor is chosen because, presumably, he/she possesses specialized knowledge, skills and experience to properly maintain or dispose of the artwork in accordance with the will's instructions.

Article of manufacture US patent law states: Whoever invents or discovers any new and useful process, machine, manufacture, or composition of matter, or any new and useful improvement thereof, may obtain a patent therefor (35 USC §101). For purposes of this definition, "manufacture" means any useful product made from raw materials directly by human labor or by machines controlled by humans (see Diamond v. Chakrabarty, 447 U.S. 303 [1980]).

Assignment The transfer of any property right, claim or interest, in its entirety, to another person or entity.

Author In copyright law, the person who created copyrightable material (see work made for hire).

Bailment A legal relationship created when one party gives property to another for safekeeping.

Business corporation A legal entity organized under state law in corporate form for the purpose of carrying on a business for profit.

Buy-sell agreement A binding contract among business partners that controls who can buy a departing partner's share of the business; what events will trigger a buyout; and what price will be paid for a partner's interest in the business (see cross-purchase buyback and entity-purchase buyback).

By-laws Rules and regulations adopted by an entity (such as a corporation or society) for its internal governance. By-laws often deal with matters such as directors and shareholders and the rights and obligations of officers. Corporate by-laws sometimes contain the company's buy-sell agreement.

Capital asset For income tax purposes, selling or exchanging a capital asset often results in favorable tax treatment. The Internal Revenue Code defines "capital asset" in the negative, i.e., by listing all the things that are not capital assets (26 USC §1221). One such category (of non-capital assets) includes: "a copyright, a literary, musical, or artistic composition, a letter or memorandum, or similar property, held by a taxpayer whose personal efforts created such property" (26 USC §1221[3][A]).

Classes In trademark law, specifically defined categories of goods and services under which one can apply for trademark registration. For a listing of all available classes, see the US Patent and Trademark Office's Trademark Manual of Examination Procedures, Chapter 1400 ("Classification and Identification of Goods and Services"), section 1401.02(a): http://www.uspto.gov/web/offices/tac/tmep/1400.htm

Compilation In copyright law, "a work formed by the collection and assembling of preexisting materials or of data that are selected, coordinated, or arranged in such a way that the resulting work as a whole constitutes an original work of authorship" (17 USC §101).

Consideration In contract law, the agreement, act, forbearance or promise of a contracting party (in simple terms: what each party "gives" and "gets"). Consideration is an essential part of a binding contract.

Consignment An arrangement whereby the owner of the goods (e.g., an artist) transfers such goods to a seller (e.g., an art gallery) who then acts as the owner's agent for purposes of selling the goods.

Convention In international law, an agreement among states or nations dealing with a specific subject, such as copyright. The document in which the agreement is memorialized is often called a **treaty**.

Copyright A bundle of exclusive rights relating to the reproduction, distribution, display, performance and creation of derivative work based upon original literary, musical, dramatic, artistic and architectural works, films, sound recordings and other statutory "work of authorship."

Cost basis The original price of an asset, plus any additions and reinvested earnings, used for income tax purposes to determine capital gain or loss at the time of the asset's sale.

Cross-purchase buyback In a buy-sell agreement, an arrangement permitting the continuing owners of the business to purchase the departing owner's interest, in proportion to their current holdings (see entity-purchase buyback).

Decedent The person who has died.

Defendant The person or entity against whom an action is brought in a court of law; the one being sued or accused

Derivative work In copyright law, a work based upon one or more preexisting works, such as a translation, musical arrangement, dramatization, fictionalization, motion picture version, sound recording, art reproduction, abridgment, condensation, or any other form in which a work may be recast, transformed, or adapted (17 USC §101).

Design patent A type of patent issued in the United States for an original design of purely ornamental or aesthetic nature made for an article of manufacture (35 USC §171). Design patents protect the appearance of an article of manufacture (rather than the article itself), from infringement.

Employer Identification Number A (usually 9-digit) number assigned by the Internal Revenue Service to identify tax-paying business entities in the United States. Also known as a federal tax identification number. For more information enter "EIN" in the search function of the IRS website: http://www.irs.gov

Entity-purchase buyback In a buy-sell agreement, an arrangement permitting the business itself (as opposed to the remaining owners) to purchase the departing owner's interest (see cross-purchase buyback).

Executor The person named in a will to carry out the will's instructions and requests. Also known as the **personal representative**. The executor pays the decedent's debts and taxes and makes distributions to beneficiaries in accordance with the instructions in the will (see also, art executor).

Exclusive license See license.

Fair market value The price at which property would change hands between a willing buyer and a willing seller, neither having to buy or sell, and both having reasonable knowledge of all relevant facts.

Fair Use A use of copyrighted material that does not constitute infringement. See Copyright Office Factsheet FL-102: http://www.copyright.gov/fls/fl102.pdf

Federal circuit courts Also called Federal courts of appeal, these courts review the final decisions of United States district courts. Decisions of the Federal circuit courts can be appealed to the United States Supreme Court.

Federal regulations A rule or order issued by a United States government agency (such as the IRS), often having the force and effect of law. Regulations must be made in accordance with prescribed procedures, such as those set out in the federal or a state Administrative Procedure Act. Federal regulations appear in the Code of Federal Regulations, or "CFR."

Financial power of attorney A legal document that authorizes one person to act as another's agent in financial and other matters, such as banking and paying bills. Typically, a financial power of attorney does not authorize the agent to make health care decisions for the principal (see health care advance directive).

First sale doctrine In copyright law, an exception to the bundle of exclusive copyright rights providing that the purchaser of copyrighted material may transfer (i.e. sell, rent, or give away) a particular, legally acquired copy of protected work without permission of the copyright owner (17 USC §109). The first sale doctrine does not apply to rental or leasing of recorded music or computer programs.

Gross estate The fair market value of everything the decedent owned or had an interest in, on the date of death. Property includible in the gross estate may consist of cash and securities, real estate, artwork, insurance, trusts, annuities, business interests and other assets.

Health care advance directive A document in which a person expresses his or her wishes regarding medical treatment in the event of incapacitation. There are two basic types of health care advance directives: a health care power of attorney and a living will. In a health care power of attorney, the principal appoints an agent to make health care decisions for him or her. In a living will, the principal expresses his or wishes regarding critical care to "the world at large" and asks that such wishes be honored.

Infringement In intellectual property law, unauthorized use or misappropriation of protected material.

Internal Revenue Code The collection of laws governing taxation in the United States, administered by the Internal Revenue Service and set forth in Title 26 of the United States Code.

Intestate succession In the absence of a will, the state-prescribed process by which a decedent's property passes to others.

Joint work In copyright law, a work prepared by two or more authors with the intention that their contributions be merged into inseparable or interdependent parts of a unitary whole. Unless there is a written agreement to the contrary, joint authors share equally in copyright ownership of the work.

Jurisdiction Three different meanings: a government's general power to exercise authority over all persons and things within its territory; a court's power to decide a case or issue a decree; and a geographic area (like a state) within which political or judicial authority may be exercised.

License Permission to commit some act that would otherwise be unlawful, such as reproducing copyrighted material. Licenses can be **exclusive** (meaning the licensor cannot grant the license to anyone other than the exclusive licensee) or **nonexclusive** (meaning the licensor may grant the same license to multiple parties). Licenses can also be revocable or irrevocable.

Limited Liability Company (LLC) An unincorporated company – statutorily authorized by state – in which owners (called members) have limited personal liability for the debts and obligations of the company. LLCs also feature management by the members or managers, limitations on ownership transfer, and the option to be taxed either as a partnership or a corporation.

Litigation The process of resolving a legal dispute in a formal court action or lawsuit.

Material breach A breach of contract substantial enough (as opposed to a **technical breach**) to allow the innocent party to pursue legal remedies.

Members See limited liability company.

Metatags Hidden HTML code that contains descriptive information about a webpage and is searchable by search engines. To view the metatags for a website (in Windows), click "View" and then "Source."

Moral rights In United States copyright law, the rights of attribution and integrity (17 USC §106A).

Nonexclusive license See license.

Notice In contract law, written warning to one party of another's intention to do something or take some (legal) action. In copyright law, an indicia placed on visually perceptible copies of works of authorship to inform the public that the work is protected by copyright. See Copyright Office Circular 3: http://www.copyright.gov/circs/circ03.pdf

Offer In contract law, a promise to do or refrain from doing some specified thing; a display of willingness to enter into a contract on specified terms, made in a way that would lead a reasonable person to understand that an acceptance will result in a binding contract (see acceptance).

Operating agreement A contract among the members of a limited liability company governing such issues as membership, management, operation and distribution of profit and loss of the company. Operating agreements often contain the members' buy-sell agreement.

Operation of law The means by which a right or a liability is created for a party regardless of the party's actual intent; this term is applied to rights and liabilities that are cast upon a party by the law, without any act by the party or a court.

Ordinary income For individual income-tax purposes, income that is derived from sources such as wages, commissions, and interest (as opposed to income from capital gains; see capital asset).

Partnership A voluntary association of two or more persons who jointly own and carry on a business for profit. Under the Uniform Partnership Act, a partnership is presumed to exist if the persons agree to share proportionally in the business's profits and losses. Unlike LLC members, general partners are personally and fully liable for all business debts and obligations of the partnership.

Patent "The right to exclude others from making, using, offering for sale, or selling" an invention in the United States or "importing" the invention into the United States. What is granted is not the right to make, use, offer for sale, sell or import, but the right to exclude others from making, using, offering for sale, selling or importing the invention.

Personal property Any movable or intangible thing that is subject to ownership and not classified as real property (see real property).

Personal representative See executor.

Plaintiff The party who brings a civil action in a court of law.

Plant patent A patent granted to one who invents or discovers and asexually reproduces any distinct and new variety of plant.

Probate property Property of a decedent that passes under the decedent's will. In contrast, property that passes "outside" of the will, such as life insurance proceeds, retirement plan benefits and other property passing by contract or operation of law, is called nonprobate property.

Pro Bono From Latin, meaning "for the public good." Uncompensated legal services performed especially for the public good.

Publication In copyright law, "the distribution of copies or phonorecords of a work to the public by sale or other transfer of ownership, or by rental, lease, or lending. The offering to distribute copies or phonorecords to a group of persons for purposes of further distribution, public performance, or public display constitutes publication. A public performance or display of a work does not of itself constitute publication." Generally, publication occurs when copies of the work are first made available to the public. If a work has not been made available to the public in this manner, it is considered unpublished.

Public domain In copyright law, any work of authorship not (or no longer) protected by copyright. This includes work published before 1923, work created for public use, and work for which the term of copyright protection has expired.

Real property Land and anything growing on, attached to, or erected on it.

Registration In copyright and trademark law, a procedure for recording one's ownership rights with a governmental agency. Registration is not required to secure legal rights, but it is necessary to pursue many related legal remedies.

Release The relinquishment of a legal right or remedy.

Revocable living trust In a trust, one party (the trustee) holds legal title to property for the benefit of another party (the beneficiary). The person who establishes a trust is called the settlor, or grantor. With a revocable living trust the grantor establishes the trust and can change its terms during his or her lifetime. The grantor lacks such power with an irrevocable trust.

Right to privacy As determined by state law, the right to be free of public embarrassment or unauthorized intrusion.

Right to publicity As determined by state law, an individual's property right in his or her own identity; the right to prevent unauthorized use of one's name or likeness for commercial benefit.

Security interest In UCC law, a property interest created by agreement or by operation of law to secure performance of an obligation.

Shareholders Individuals or entities that own stock in a corporation.

Signatory In international law, a nation that joins a convention or treaty.

Statute An act of the legislature; another word for a "law."

Statutory damages Damages that are set in amount by the legislature, for particularly offensive violations of the law. Typically, if they meet certain prerequisites, plaintiffs can collect statutory damages without proving actual losses.

Strict liability Liability imposed upon a defendant even when there is no proof of negligence.

Summary judgment A final judgment granted before trial on a claim about which a judge has determined there is no genuine issue of material fact, and upon which the movant (the party requesting summary judgment) is entitled to prevail as a matter of law. On one hand, this procedural device allows the speedy disposition of issues without the need for trial. On the other hand, if you are the party against whom summary judgment has been granted, you lose the opportunity for trial and your only remedy is to appeal the judgment.

Tax-exempt Not subject to taxation.

Technical breach See material breach.

Testamentary trust A trust established in one's will (see revocable living trust).

Trade dress A product's design, product packaging, color, or other distinguishing nonfunctional element of appearance.

Trademark A distinctive word, phrase, logo, or other symbol used by a manufacturer or seller to distinguish its goods and services from those of others.

Treaty See convention.

United States Code A consolidation and codification by subject matter of the general and permanent laws of the United States.

Unpublished See publication.

Utility patent Patent protection granted to one who "invents or discovers any new and useful process, machine, article of manufacture, or composition of matter, or any new and useful improvement thereof" (see article of manufacture).

Will A written and signed statement, made by an individual, providing upon death for the disposition of his or her probate property, guardianship of his or her children and payment of his or her debts and obligations (see probate property).

Work of authorship In copyright law: literary works; musical works, including any accompanying words; dramatic works, including any accompanying music; pantomimes and choreographic works; pictorial, graphic, and sculptural works; motion pictures and other audiovisual works; sound recordings; and architectural works (17 USC § 102).

Work made for hire In copyright law, an exception to the general rule that the person who creates a work of authorship is its author. A work qualifying as "work made for hire" is a work prepared by an employee within the scope of his or her employment; or a work specially ordered or commissioned in certain specified circumstances. When a work qualifies as a work made for hire, the employer, or commissioning party, is considered to be the author.

D

E

F

U

V

W

About the Author

 lizabeth T Russell is a frequent lecturer on legal issues for artists, musicians and nonprofit organizations. She received the world's only known bassoon scholarship to law school, and is admitted to practice law in the states of New York, Connecticut and Wisconsin.

 Early in her career Ms. Russell served as a senior attorney in the Counsel's Office of the New York State Education Department. During her tenure there she represented the New York State Museum in negotiations leading to the repatriation of twelve sacred wampum belts to the Onondaga Nation. She also represented the Commissioner of Education in litigation before the United States Supreme Court.

Following her public service, Ms. Russell took a sabbatical from the practice of law in order to work in the arts. She held positions with the Albany Symphony Orchestra in Albany, NY; the Madison Repertory Theatre in Madison, WI; and Opera for the Young, a professional opera company. These experiences provided her with a first-hand understanding of the artistic community's legal needs.

Ms. Russell returned to law in 2000 and opened her own firm, concentrating in arts and entertainment, copyright, trademark, business and nonprofit law. Every day, her practical experiences in the arts inform her legal work with artists, musicians and business clients in the arts and entertainment industry.

Elizabeth Russell is a member of the Entertainment, Arts and Sports Law section of the New York State Bar Association; the Sports and Entertainment Law section of the State Bar of Wisconsin and the Copyright Society of the United States.

ORDER FORM

STANDARD COPIES:
$16.95 *(each)*

PERSONALIZED COPIES:
$21.95 *(each)*

SHIPPING VIA U.S. MAIL:
$3.00 + $1 each
additional book

OVERNIGHT SHIPPING AVAILABLE
(phone orders only)

(rp) Ruly Press

Ruly Press
402 Gammon Place, Suite 270
Madison, WI 53719
Fax: 608-833-1566
Phone: 608-833-1555
www.rulypress.com

ART LAW CONVERSATIONS
By Elizabeth T Russell

Qty	Standard or Personalized	Recipient's Name *(for personalized copies) Please print*	Price	Total
____	_____	_____	____	____
____	_____	_____	____	____
____	_____	_____	____	____
____	_____	_____	____	____

	Subtotal:	____
	Sales tax @5.5%: *(WI residents only)*	____
	Shipping:	____
	TOTAL:	____

CUSTOMER INFORMATION

Name _____

Company _____

Street Address _____

City_____ State _____ Zip_____

Phone (_____)_____ Fax (_____)_____

Email _____

PAYMENT METHOD

☐ Check enclosed ☐ VISA ☐ MasterCard

Credit card # _____ Exp. Date_____

COMMENTS

_____

_____

TALK TO US

Conversations With You

WE WANT TO KNOW WHAT YOU THINK. REALLY.

rp Ruly Press

402 Gammon Place, Suite 270
Madison, WI 53719
Fax: 608-833-1566
Email: tsdams@rulypress.com

HOW DID YOU HEAR ABOUT ART LAW CONVERSATIONS?

_____

_____

_____

_____

_____

WHAT DID YOU THINK ABOUT THE BOOK?

_____

_____

_____

_____

WHAT OTHER TOPICS WOULD YOU LIKE US TO PUBLISH?

_____

_____

_____

_____

NOBODY'S PERFECT!

Please let us know how we can improve future editions of this book.

22'⁵

Received
FEB 8 2007
Mission College Library